Dependency Injection In Delphi

Nick Hodges

Dependency Injection In Delphi

Nick Hodges

ISBN 978-1-941266-22-9

Dependency Injection in Delphi

ISBN 978-1-941266-22-9

Published by: Trenchant Publishing PO Box 314 Pottstown, PA 19464

Also By Nick Hodges

Coding In Delphi

More Coding in Delphi

To my wonderful, beautiful wife Pamela. I love you.

Contents

Preface

Why a whole book about Dependency Injection (DI) in Delphi, especially since I wrote about it in my first book *Coding in Delphi*?

Well, there are a few reasons why.

First, I see now that *Coding in Delphi* just scratched the surface of what Dependency Injection is and how to do it properly. That's not to say that the information in it isn't useful, but a lot has changed in the last few years with regard to DI, and I've also learned a lot in the intervening years. This book aims to bring you up to date with the latest developments in Dependency Injection using Delphi.

Second, there have been a number of very powerful new features added to the Spring for Delphi Dependency Injection container that need to be discussed. Stefan Gleinke, the maintainer and developer of Spring4D, has not been idle, and he's added a lot to the Container over the last few years. His great work deserves further attention.

And third, I want to write this book because I still see people making fledgling attempts at doing Dependency Injection and they struggle to do it well. I see them trying to use it to manage their forms – something I do not recommend. I see them not applying basic DI and jumping right in to using the DI Container in Spring4D before understanding why and how to use it. And when they do use a container, they try to force things into it that don't belong there. This all begs to be explained and corrected.

This book exists to address all those issues. My first goal is to cover the topic thoroughly and completely – top to bottom, left to right, and front to back. I intend to do that by explaining everything there is to know about Dependency Injection. My second goal is to show you the proper use of a DI container, as well as show you how not to use it, and demonstrate these things using the Spring4D Container. And finally, I would like this book to become the final word for Delphi developers on how to do Dependency Injection.

Dependency Injection is actually the simplest thing in the world, but sometimes it takes a lot of work to grasp simple things. I can say un-ashamedly that I know a lot more about it than I did when I wrote about it in my first book. There I dedicated only two chapters to the topic. Here I will dedicate a whole book to it. I will endeavor to help "the light bulb to go on" about Dependency Injection, so that its use becomes second nature to you. I'll help you see the anti-patterns that are all too commonly used, and I'll show you the proper patterns for building loosely coupled applications.

Most of the material in this book will be new. I will not use the same examples from *Coding in Delphi*, but you may see some of the same principles discussed in that book also covered here.

I think it is also important to note that this is really a book about Dependency Injection that happens to use Delphi as the language for the demos. At least, I want it to be that. The principles discussed herein are true for any development language, and so if you are by chance a C# developer or a user of some language other than Object Pascal who is reading this, fear not. Delphi code is easy to read and understand, and you should be able to learn all I have to say without knowing a lick of Delphi.

This book is divided into two parts: One that discusses Dependency Injection, and the other that discusses the use of what is commonly called a DI Container. DI does not require the use of a container, as I will stress many times going forward.

This book will also make extensive use of the Spring for Delphi Framework. I'll use Spring4D's DI Container, the `Guard` class, and maybe some of the collections. If you haven't added Spring4D to your arsenal, you should do so immediately. Its excellent implementation of generic, interfaced-based collections alone is worth it. The Spring4D Framework can be found at http://www.spring4d.org.

The code for this book is available at this link: http://bit.ly/diidcode

All the code in this book was written and compiled with Delphi 10.1 Berlin. I can't promise that it will work in any previous version, but I don't see why it wouldn't.

Okay, so let's get to it. You have nothing to lose but your spaghetti code.

Nick Hodges

Gilbertsville, PA

February, 2017

Acknowledgements

First, I'd like to say thank you to my wife, Pamela, who supported this effort from start to finish.

I'd like to thank Baoquan Zuo who originally wrote the Spring for Delphi framework, including the Dependency Injection Container. Your contributions to the Delphi community are many and much appreciated.

I'd also like to thank Stefan Glienke for all his great work in maintaining the Spring for Delphi after taking it over from Baoquan. Without you, we wouldn't have the Spring for Delphi framework as it is today.

In addition, I am deeply indebted to Stefan for his careful and thorough technical review of this book. It is vastly better as a result.

Bruce McGee graciously read the rough draft and provided invaluable feedback that improved the book greatly. I am grateful for his help.

What is Dependency Injection?

Introduction

I have three kids. They are older now, but when they were younger, it was fun to bake with them. We'd bake a cake or cookies or some other confection that they would then enjoy eating. But there was one problem – we made a huge mess when we baked. There was flour and sugar and all kinds of stuff all over the place and all over us. The process of baking left us with a big job of cleaning up. It made for a lot of work. Sure, we had fun, but the mess was there, nonetheless.

How to avoid the mess? Well, we could be more careful, I suppose, but kids will be kids. Oftentimes, we would be baking a birthday cake. An alternative, of course, to all of the hassle and mess of baking a cake would be to go to the store and buy a pre-made cake. An even better solution would be to find a bakery that would deliver birthday cakes to order, dropping off at your doorstep exactly what you wanted for your birthday cake.

Now here is something else to consider. Say the delivery guy shows up and he's been tromping through mud and his boots are filthy, and he's got a vicious cough. Are you going to let him into your house? No – of course not. You'd probably take one look at him through the crack in the door and tell him to put the cake box down on the porch and get the heck off your lawn. You'd be awfully careful about the cake, too, I guess, but for the sake of argument we'll assume it is well wrapped and protected from whatever phlegm the delivery guy was emitting. In other words, you'd want your interaction with the delivery person to be as minimal as possible, but you still want the cake. Your kid is going to be pretty upset if he or she doesn't get to blow out the candles on their birthday cake. You want the cake without the mess and with the thinnest of interactions with the delivery person.

One might even say that you had a dependency on a birthday cake, and the bakery was injecting that dependency by delivering the cake to you. Hmm.

Or let's say you are at the supermarket, and you have a grocery cart full of groceries. You take them to the checkout guy, and he rings them all up. He says "That'll be $123.45." So what do you do? Do you hand him your wallet and have him dig around for cash or a credit card? Of course not – you want to keep the interaction as minimal as possible with your wallet – you don't want him rooting around in it. Who knows what will happen. Instead, you give the guy cash, or you pull out your credit card and hand it to him. Or better yet, you swipe the card yourself so that the checkout guy never even touches your card. Again, you want to have that interaction be as minimal as possible. You might say that you want to keep the interface between you and the clerk to a minimum.

One more. Say you are looking at buying a house. You search all over town and you finally find a place that you really like. Good location, good school district, good neighborhood. Only there is one problem – all the electrical devices are hard-wired into the house. All the lamps, the toaster, the hair-dryer, everything is hard-wired. There are no plugs in the house. Everything is wired directly into the electrical system, so you can't easily replace anything. The normal interfaces – electrical plugs – between the electrical devices and the electrical system simply are not there. You couldn't replace your toaster without calling an electrician. One might say that the lack of interfaces has made things very difficult to deal with, and thus you decide not to buy the house.

Are you seeing a pattern here?

Okay, enough stories. I'll just say it. In your code, the interaction between objects should be as thin and clean as possible. You should ask for precisely what you need and nothing more. If you need something, you should ask for it – have it "delivered" to you – instead of trying to create it yourself. That way, just like with the cake and the cashier and the house, things stay neat and clean and flexible. I think code that is neat and clean and flexible sounds pretty good.

That is the essence of Dependency Injection. It's really nothing more than that. Dependency Injection is a twenty-five dollar term for a ten cent concept: If you need something, ask for it. Don't create things yourself – push that off to someone else. Every class of any substance will likely need help from other classes. If your class needs help, ask for it; don't try to "do it yourself." Remember, every time you try to "do it yourself" you create a hard-coded dependency. And again, those should be avoided like global variables.

It is, as we shall see, really that simple.

One thing to notice – and this is a point I'll harp on throughout the first part of the book – is that we haven't yet used the word "Container". In fact, here's a tweet of mine:

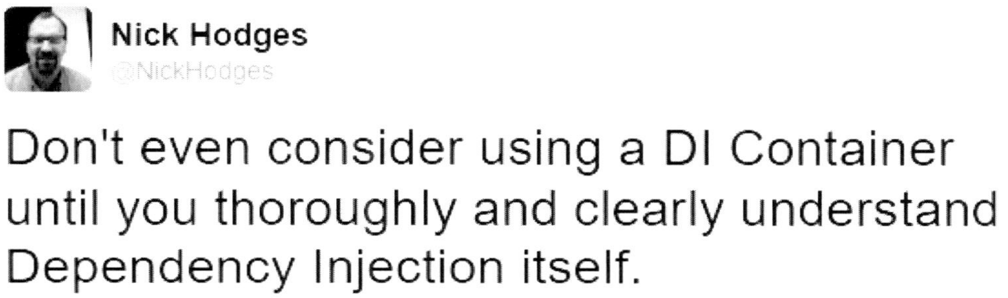

A really wise tweet

That may sound a bit weird, but it makes an important point: "Doing Dependency Injection" and "Using a Dependency Injection container" are really two very different things. They are related – the latter making the former easier to scale – but they are ***not*** the same thing. In fact, I'll cover a lot of territory before I talk about the DI Container again.

So What Exactly is Dependency Injection?

By now you probably are wondering what DI exactly is. Well, according to Mark Seemann, author of the wonderful book "Dependency Injection in .Net", Dependency Injection is "a set of software design principles and patterns that enable us to develop loosely coupled code." That's a good definition, but a bit antiseptic. Let's explore a bit more deeply.

If you are going to inject a dependency, you need to know what a dependency is. A dependency is anything that a given class needs to do its job, such as fields, other classes, etc. If `TClassA` needs `TClassB` to be present to compile, then it `TClassA` is dependent on `TClassB`. Or in other words, `TClassB` is a dependency of `TClassA`. Dependencies get created when, well, you create one. Here's an example:

```
type

  TClassB = class
  end;

  TClassA = class
  private
    FClassB: TClassB;
  public
    constructor Create;
  end;

constructor TClassA.Create;
begin
  FClassB := TClassB.Create;
end;
```

In the above code, we have created a hard-coded dependency to `TClassB` in `TClassA`. It's just like the hair dryer or the toaster discussed earlier – it is hard-wired into the class. `TClassA` is completely dependent on `TClassB`. `TClassB` is "coupled" to `TClassA`. Tightly coupled. About as tightly coupled as you can get, really. And tight coupling is bad.

A Word About Coupling

As we've seen above, coupling is the notion of one thing being dependent on another. Tight coupling is when things ***really*** depend on each other and are strictly tied. You can't compile class `A` without the complete definition of class `B` being present. `B` is permanently stuck to `A`. Tight coupling is bad – it creates inflexible code. Think how hard it would be to move around if you were hand-cuffed to another person. That's how a class feels when you create hard-coded dependencies.

What you want is to keep the coupling between your classes and modules as "loose" as possible. That is, you want your dependencies to be as thin as you can make them. If you have a class that needs a customer name, pass in just the customer name. Don't pass in the entire customer. And as we shall see, if your class needs another class, pass in an abstraction – an interface, usually – of that class. An interface is like a wisp of smoke – there is something there, but you really can't grab on to it.

> This notion is so important that we'll discuss it more fully in the next chapter.

How do you create these hard-coded, tightly coupled dependencies? You create them by, well, creating things inside other classes. Look at the example above. The constructor of `TClassA` creates an instance of `TClassB` and stores it internally. That `Create` call creates the dependency. You need `TClassB` to compile `TClassA`.

What to Do?

Well, the first thing to do is not to create `TClassB` inside `TClassA`. Instead, "inject" the dependency via the constructor:

```
type

  TClassB = class
  end;

  TClassA = class
  private
    FClassB: TClassB;
  public
    constructor Create(aClassB: TClassB);
  end;

constructor TClassA.Create(aClassB: TClassB);
begin
  FClassB := aClassB;
end;
```

By doing this, you loosen the coupling up a bit. First note that you can now pass in any instance of `TClassB` that you want. You can even pass in a descendent if that makes sense. You are still tied to `TClassB`, and `TClassA` still cannot be compiled without `TClassB`, but you've added some flexibility by loosening the coupling just a touch. `TClassA` and `TClassB` are still coupled, but they are more loosely coupled.

> So at this point, we have two types of coupling: one where the first class actually creates an instance of the second class and one where the first class needs the second class, i.e. where it is injected. The latter is

> preferable to the former in that it involves less (looser) coupling. In the next chapter we'll take a look at the hierarchy of coupling – a concept called "connascence."

And that, friends, is the essence of DI. Inject your dependencies instead of creating them. That's it. That's Dependency Injection. I could stop right here, and if that were the only thing I taught you, your code would be better off than it is today (because, face it, your code base is *full* of hard-coded dependencies, right?). I could end the book right here and you'd have a new tool in your tool chest that would really improve things.

But, of course, it really isn't that simple. There's more to it than that, and as projects scale up, things get complicated, but as a first example, it goes a long way towards describing what DI is and how it works. In the coming chapters, we'll explore it more deeply, but if you've understood and seen the power of this simple technique, you are well on your way to writing better, cleaner, easier to maintain, and more flexible code.

Basic Principles to Follow

There are a few underlying principles that will pervade this book and have bearing on the topic of Dependency Injection. They are as follows:

Code Against Abstractions, Not Implementations

Erich Gamma of the "Gang of Four" (the authors of the book "Design Patterns") is credited with coining this phrase, and it is a powerful and essential idea. If you teach new developers only one thing, it should be this aphorism. Abstractions – usually interfaces but not always (see below) – are flexible. Interfaces (or abstract classes) can be implemented in many ways. Interfaces can be coded against before the implementation is even completed. If you code to an implementation, you are creating a tightly coupled and inflexible system. Don't lock yourself into a single implementation. Instead, use abstractions and allow your code to be supple, reusable, and flexible.

Never Create Things that Shouldn't Be Created

Your classes should follow the Single Responsibility Principle – the idea that a class should only do one thing. If they do that, then they shouldn't be creating things, because that makes two things that they are doing. Instead, they should ask for the functionality that they need and let something else create and provide that functionality.

Creatables vs. Injectables

So what should be created? Well, there are two different kinds of objects that we should concern ourselves with: "Creatables" and "Injectables."

Creatables are classes that you should go ahead and create. They are RTL or utility classes that are common and well-known. For Delphi developers, these are things like `TStringList` and `TList<T>`. Generally, classes in the Delphi runtime should be considered Creatables. Classes like this should not be injected, but should be created by your classes. They often have short lifetimes, frequently living no longer than the span of a single method. If they are required by the class as a whole, they can be created in the constructor. One should pass only other Creatables to the constructor of a Creatable.

Injectables, on the other hand, are classes that we never want to create directly. They are the types of classes that we never want to hard-code a dependency to and that should always be passed via Dependency Injection. They normally will be asked for as dependencies in a constructor. Following the rule above, injectables should be referenced via interfaces and not direct references to an instance. Injectables will most often be classes that you write as part of your business logic. They should always be hidden behind an abstraction, usually an interface. Note, too, that injectables can ask for other injectables in their constructor.

Keep Constructors Simple

Constructors should be kept simple. The constructor of a class should not be doing any "work" – that is, they shouldn't be doing anything other than checking for nil, creating Creatables, and storing dependencies for later use. They should not include any coding logic. An 'if' clause in a class's constructor that isn't checking for `nil` is a cry for that class to be split into two classes. (There are ways to check for nil value parameters that don't involve an `if` statement. We'll cover the notion of "Never accept `nil`" in a later chapter.) A complex constructor is a clear sign that your class is doing too much. Keep constructors short, simple, and free of any logic.

Don't Assume Anything About the Implementation

Interfaces are, of course, useless without an implementation. However, you as a developer should never make any assumptions about what that implementation is. You should only code against the contract made by the interface. You may have written the implementation, but you shouldn't code against the interface with that implementation in mind. Put another way, code against your interface as if a radically new and better implementation of that interface is right around the corner. A well-designed interface will tell you what you need to do and how it is to be used. The implementation of that interface should be immaterial to your usage of the interface.

Don't Assume That an Interface is an Abstraction

Interfaces are nice, and I certainly sing their praises all the time. However, it is important to realize that not every interface is an abstraction. For instance, if your interface is an exact representation of the public portion of your class, you really aren't "abstracting" anything, right? (Such interfaces are called "header interfaces" because they resemble C++ header files). Interfaces extracted from classes can easily be tightly coupled to that class alone, making the interface useless as an abstraction. Finally, abstractions can be "leaky," that is, they can reveal specific implementation details about their implementation. Leaky abstractions are also normally tied to a specific implementation. (You can read more about this notion in an excellent blog post by Mark Seemann at [http://bit.ly/2awOhmn]http://bit.ly/2awOhmn).)

Conclusion

Okay, so that should serve as a basic introduction to the idea of Dependency Injection. Dependency Injection is a means to an end, and that end is loosely coupled code.

Obviously there is more to it than that, hence the rest of this book. But if you understand the notions that you should code against abstractions and that you should ask for the functionality that you need, you are well on your way to understanding Dependency Injection and to writing better code.

Benefits of Dependency Injection

Why should we do all this? Why go to all the trouble to arrange our code in the particular way called for by the principles of Dependency Injection? Well, because there are benefits. Let's talk a bit about those benefits of Dependency Injection, because they are many and compelling.

Maintainability – Probably the main benefit of Dependency Injection is maintainability. If your classes are loosely coupled and follow the single responsibility principle – the natural result of using DI – then your code will be easier to maintain. Simple, stand-alone classes are easier to fix than complicated, tightly coupled classes. Code that is maintainable has a lower total cost of ownership. Maintenance costs often exceed the cost of building the code in the first place, so anything that improves the maintainability of your code is a good thing. We all want to save time and money, right?

Testability – Along the same lines as maintainability is testability. Code that is easy to test is tested more often. More testing means higher quality. Loosely coupled classes that only do one thing – again, the natural result of using DI – are very easy to unit test. By using Dependency Injection, you make creating test doubles (commonly called "mocks") much easier. If dependencies are passed to classes, it's quite simple to pass in a test double implementation. If dependencies are hard-coded, it's impossible to create test doubles for those dependencies. Testable code that actually is tested is quality code. Or at least it's of higher quality than untested code. I find it hard to accept the argument that unit tests are a waste of time – they are always worth the time to me. (Surely I'm not the only one who finds it strange that this is even in dispute?)

Readability – Code that uses DI is simpler. It follows the Single Responsibility Principle and thus results in smaller, more compact and to the point classes. Constructors aren't as cluttered and filled with logic. Classes are more clearly defined, openly declaring what they need. Because of all this, DI-based code is more readable. And code that is more readable is more maintainable.

Flexibility – Loosely couple code – yet again, the result of using DI – is more flexible and usable in different ways. Small classes that do one thing can more easily be reassembled and reused in different situations. Small classes are like Legos(tm) – they can easily be pieced together to make a multitude of things, as opposed to say, Duplo(tm) blocks, which are bulkier and less flexible. Being able to reuse code saves time and money. All software needs to be able to change and adapt to new requirements. Loosely coupled code that uses Dependency Injection is flexible and able to adapt to those changes.

Extensibility – Code that uses Dependency Injection results in a class structure that is more extendable. By relying on abstractions instead of implementations, code can easily vary a given implementation. When you code against abstractions, you can code with the notion that a radically better implementation of what you are doing is just around the corner. Small, flexible classes can be extended easily, either by inheritance or composition. An application's code base never remains static, and you will very likely need to add new features as your code base grows and new requirements arise. Code that is extensible is up to that challenge.

Team Development – If you are on a team and that team needs to work together on a project (when is that not true?), then Dependency Injection will facilitate team development. (Even if you are working alone, it is very likely that your work will be passed to someone in the future). Dependency Injection calls for you to code against abstractions and not implementations. If you have two teams working together, each needing the other's work, you can define the abstractions before doing the implementations, and then each team can write their code using the abstractions, even before the implementations are written. In addition, because code is loosely coupled, those implementations won't rely on each other, and thus they are easily split between teams.

So there you have it. Dependency Injection results in maintainable, testable, readable, flexible, and extensible code that is easily spread between team members. It seems hard to imagine that any developer wouldn't want all that.

A Closer Look at Coupling: Connascence

Introduction

If you've been paying attention, you've noticed that I don't like coupling. Tightly coupled code makes me queasy. I talk about it in my blog posts, in my books, everywhere. Tight coupling is bad. We know that we want loose coupling and should avoid tight coupling. That's sort of been a given, but there has been precious little discussion of exactly what it all means. It's been notoriously hard to describe. It's been an "I know it when I see it" kind of thing. Since Dependency Injection is all about reducing coupling, I thought it would be a good idea to include this chapter covering a bit more about what coupling is.

Coupling is a measure of the relationships and connections between two modules. Code has to be coupled somehow or else it can't do anything. But how are those measurements taken? What exactly *is* being measured? These are tough questions. Given that tight coupling is bad, we want to limit it as much as possible. But how, exactly, do we do that? What the heck ***is*** coupling *exactly*?

Connascence

Luckily, there is a way to measure coupling. It's called "connascence." (I've heard it pronounced "Cuh-NAY-since") In the realm of software development, two modules are said to be "connascent" if changing one requires a change in the other in order to maintain the overall correctness of the system. That's pretty much what we think of when we think of coupling. The term was first used in this way by Meilir Page-Jones for the purpose of being able to quantify and qualify exactly what coupling is. He first discussed it in his book "What Every Programmer Should Know About Object-Oriented Design". The book was published in 1995, so this notion is nothing new. However, as is often the case, this twenty-year old idea is only now coming into the fore. Connascence is a way of measuring the coupling in your code.

Connascence is discussed in two dimensions. First, there are nine different levels of connascence. Second, those levels all have certain qualities. I'll discuss those qualities first, and then we'll move on to talk about the levels of connascence. The levels of connascence allow us to form a taxonomy of coupling and give us a vocabulary for talking about it. This is really useful, as previously discussions of coupling generally fell into a very amorphous discussion about "tight vs. loose" – hardly a scientific view of things.

Qualities of Connascence

Connascence has three qualities: Strength, Degree, and Locality.

Strength of Connascence

One level of connascence is said to be stronger than another if fixing it requires more in depth and more difficult changes. For instance, if reducing the coupling between two entities requires an easy, simple change, then the connascence is said to be less strong than connascence requiring a complex change. If a level of connascence is hard to refactor, it is said to be a strong level of connascence. The Levels of Connascence described below are listed by increasing strength. That ordering gives you an idea of how to prioritize your refactoring. That is, you should work to refactor the strongest couplings down to weaker levels of coupling.

Degree of Connascence

The degree of connascence is a measure of the level to which the connascence occurs. Connascence can occur to a small degree or a large degree. For example, two modules might be connected by multiple references as opposed to a single reference. A connection of multiple references is said to have a high degree of connascence. A given method might have many parameters which couple it to many external classes. Such a method has a high degree of connascence.

Locality of Connascence

Sometimes coupling occurs close together – you have two classes in the same unit that are interconnected. Connascence can occur within a single method. But sometimes that coupling occurs in two units that are very far apart from each other. We've all seen this – you make a change in the "lower left" part of your application and it has an effect far away in the "upper right" of the program. Connascence that is close together is better than that which is far apart.

Levels of Connascence

Some coupling is required. Without it, nothing can happen in an application. However, we want to keep the strength of coupling as weak as possible, the degree as small as possible, and the locality as close as possible. If we could measure the coupling, then we could know that we are doing that, right? Well, Page-Jones described nine levels of connascence, each stronger, of higher degree, and/or of more distant locality than the previous one. Once we recognize these levels of coupling, we can do things to reduce them to a lower level. Let's take a look and see how it all works.

Static Connascenses

The first five levels of Connascenses are said to be static because they can be found by visually examining your code.

Connascence of Name

Connascence of Name occurs when two things have to agree on the name of something. This is the weakest form of connascence, and the one that we should aspire to limit ourselves to. It's almost obvious, and can't be avoided. If you declare a procedure:

```
procedure TMyClass.DoSomething
```

you have to call it using the name `DoSomething`. Changing the name of something requires changes elsewhere. If you want to change the name of the procedure, you need to change it everywhere that you've called it. That seems obvious, and of course this level of connascence is unavoidable. In fact, it's desirable. It's the lowest level of coupling we can have, and so we should seek it out and use it the most. If we can limit our coupling to Connascence of Name, we'd be doing very well.

Connascence of Type

Connascence of Type occurs when two entities have to agree on the type of something. The most obvious example is the parameters of a method. If you declare a function as follows:

```
function TSomeClass.ProcessWidget(aWidget: TWidget; aAction: TWidgetActionType): Boolean;
```

then any calling code must pass a `TWidget` and a `TWidgetActionType` as parameters of the `ProcessWidget` function and must accept a `Boolean` as a result type. Delphi is strongly typed, so this type of connascence is almost always caught by the compiler. Connascence of Type isn't quite as weak as Connascence of Name, but it is still considered a weak and acceptable level of connascence. Indeed, you couldn't really get along without it, could you – you have to be able to call a method of a class to get anything done, and it's not very burdensome to ensure that your types match. In fact, in Delphi, you have to couple code via Connascence of Type to even compile your code.

Connascence of Meaning

Connascence of Meaning occurs when components must agree on the meaning of particular values. Connascence of Meaning most often occurs when we use "magic numbers", that is, a specific value that has meaning and that is used in multiple places. Consider the following code:

```
function GetWidgetType(aWidget: TWidget): integer;
begin
  if aWidget.Status = 'Working' then
  begin
    Result := 1;
  end else
  begin
    if aWidget.Status = 'Broken' then
    begin
      Result := 2;
    end else
    begin
      if aWidget.State = 'Missing' then
      begin
        Result := 3;
      end else
      begin
        Result := 0;
      end;
    end;
  end;
end;
```

If you want to use the above code, then you have to know the meaning of the result code for the `GetWidgetType` function. If you change one of the result types or add a new one, then you need to change the code that uses this function wherever it is used. And to make that change, you have to know the meaning of each result code.

The obvious solution here is to refactor the code to use constant names for the result code, or better, an enumerated type that defines the result codes. This reduces your connascence from Connascence of Meaning to Connascence of Name, a desirable outcome. Remember, any time you can refactor from a higher to a lower level of connascence, you have lowered coupling and thus improved your code.

Another example of Connascence of Meaning is the use of `nil` as a signal. Often, developers use `nil` to mean "no value" or "Sorry, I couldn't do/find/complete that," and your code has to handle that. As we'll see in later chapters, this use of `nil` should be avoided as it creates coupling via the Connascence of Meaning.

Connascence of Position

Connascence of Position occurs when code in two different places must agree on the position of things. This most commonly occurs in parameter lists where the order of parameters in a method's parameter list is required to maintain that order. If you add a parameter in the middle of an existing parameter list, all uses of that method must add the new parameter in the correct position.

Some languages allow you to name your parameters so that they can be included in any order, but Delphi doesn't allow this. Thus, it is required to couple code using Connascence of Position when writing Delphi code.

Now, the degree of your Connascence of Position can be reduced by limiting the number of parameters in any given routine. To limit Connascence of Position, you can reduce a parameter list to a single type, thus moving from Connascence of Position to Connascence of Type. Connascence of Type is a weaker coupling, and so this is something you should try to do.

Here's an example. Consider this routine:

```
procedure TUserManager.AddUser(aFirstName: string; aLastName: string; aAge: integer; aBirthdate: TDate\
Time; aAddress: TAddress; aPrivileges: TPrivileges);
```

In order to use `AddUser` you have to make sure that you get all the parameters in exactly the right position. If you add a parameter in the middle, you need to make sure that any use of `AddUser` puts that new value in exactly the right place.

We can reduce this example of Connascence of Position by refactoring it to use Connascence of Type instead. For example:

```
type
  TUserRecord = record
    FirstName: string;
    LastName: string;
    Age: integer;
    Birthday: TDateTime;
    Address: TAddress;
    Privileges: TPrivileges;
  end;

procedure TUserManager.AddUser(aUser: TUserRecord);
```

Now we have reduced the coupling by creating a type and having the `AddUser` procedure depend on the type of the parameter instead of the position of a long list of parameters. By reducing the strength of the coupling, we've improved the code. This technique is also referred to as a "Parameter Object." (See http://refactoring.com/catalog/introduceParameterObject.html)

Connascence of Algorithm

Connascence of Algorithm occurs when two modules must agree on a specific algorithm in order to function together.

Imagine you had a system that had a C# based API that was to be consumed by a Delphi client. The information sent between these two modules is sensitive and must be encrypted. Thus, these two modules are coupled by Connascence of Algorithm because both must agree on the encryption algorithm that will be used. If the sender changes the encryption algorithm, the receiver must change to the same algorithm.

Reducing Connascence of Algorithm is difficult, because it most often has a high degree of locality (that is, the coupling occurs far away). One solution might be to create a single module that becomes the one place where the algorithm is found and then have both consuming modules use that single module.

Dynamic Connascenses

The next four levels of connascence are said to be "dynamic" because they can only be discovered by running your code. These levels are stronger than the static ones because they only reveal themselves at runtime, making them hard to spot and very often harder to fix.

Connascence of Execution

Connascence of Execution occurs when the order of execution of code is required for the system to be correct. It is often referred to as "Temporal Coupling."

Here's an example using the code from above:

```
UserRecord.FirstName := 'Alicia';
UserRecord.LastName := 'Florrick';
UserRecord.Age = 47;
UserManager.AddUser(UserRecord);
UserRecord.Birthday := EncodeDate(1968, 12, 3);
```

This code adds the `Birthday` value ***after*** the user has been added. This clearly won't work. Obviously this is noticeable by examining the code, but you could imagine a more complex scenario that was harder to spot. Consider this code:

```
SprocketProcesser.AddSprocket(SomeSprocket);
SprocketProcessor.ValidateSprocket;
```

Does the order of those two statements matter? Does the sprocket need to be added and then validated, or should it be validated before it is added? It is hard to say, and someone not well versed in the system might make the mistake of putting them in the wrong order. That is Connascense of Execution.

Here's another example. Imagine a queue that holds messages. The first message says "Start list". Then the next two messages have list items in them for adding items to the list. Then, finally, the queue has a message that says "End list". This works great if you have a single worker thread pulling items out of the queue. All the items will be pulled out in order. But what if you had multiple threads pulling items out of the queue, and one of the threads worked a bit faster than the others, and then it pulled the "End list" message off of the queue before the final "Here's another item" message was processed? That would be bad. That would also be an error caused by Connascense of Execution.

Connascence of Timing

Connascence of Timing occurs when the timing of execution makes a difference in the outcome of the application. The most obvious example of this is a threaded race condition, where two threads pursue the same resource, and only one of the threads can win the race. Connascence of Timing is notoriously difficult to find and diagnose, and it can reveal itself in unpredictable ways.

Connascence of Value

Connascence of Value occurs when several values must be properly coordinated between modules. For instance, imagine you have a unit test that looks like this:

```
[Test]
procedure TestCheckoutValue;
var
  PriceScanner: IPriceScanner;
begin
  PriceScanner := TPriceScanner.Create;
  PriceScanner.Scan('Frosted Sugar Bombs');
  Assert.Equals(50, PriceScanner.CurrentBalance);
end;
```

So we've written the test. Now, in the spirit of Test Driven Development, I'll make the test pass as easily and simply as possible.

```
procedure TPriceScanner.Scan(aItem: string);
begin
  CurrentBalance := 50;
end;
```

We now have tight coupling between `TPriceScanner` and our test. We obviously have Connascense of Name, because both classes rely on the name `CurrentBalance`. But that's relatively low level, and perfectly acceptable. We have Connascence of Type, because both must agree on the type `TPriceScanner`, but again, that's benign. We have Connascence of Meaning, because both routines have a hard coded dependency on the number 50. That should be refactored. But the real problem is the Connascence of Value that occurs because both of the classes know the price – that is, the "Value" – for the price of Frosted Sugar Bombs. If the price changes, even our very simple test will break.

The solution is to refactor to a lower level of connascence. The first thing you could do is to refactor so that the knowledge of the price (the value) of the Frosted Sugar Bombs is maintained in only one place:

```
procedure TPriceScanner.Scan(aItem: string; aPrice: integer);
begin
  CurrentBalance := aPrice;
end;
```

and now our test can read as follows:

```
[Test]
procedure TestCheckoutValue;
var
  PriceScanner: IPriceScanner;
begin
  PriceScanner := TPriceScanner.Create;
  PriceScanner.Scan('Frosted Sugar Bombs', 50);
  Assert.Equals(50, PriceScanner.CurrentBalance);
end;
```

And we now no longer have Connascence of Value between the two modules and our test still passes. Excellent.

Connascence of Identity

Connascence of Identity occurs when two components must refer to the same object. If the two modules refer to the same thing, and then one changes that reference, the other object must change to the same reference. It's often a subtle and difficult to detect form of connascence. As a result, this is the most complex form of connascence.

Consider the following code:

```
program Identity;

{$APPTYPE CONSOLE}

{$R *.res}

uses
  System.SysUtils;

type
  TReportInfo = class
  private
    FReportStuff: string;
    procedure SetReportStuff(const Value: string);
  public
    property ReportStuff: string read FReportStuff write SetReportStuff;
  end;

procedure TReportInfo.SetReportStuff(const Value: string);
begin
  FReportStuff := Value;
end;

type
  TInventoryReport = class
```

```
  private
    FReportInfo: TReportInfo;
  public
    constructor Create(aReportInfo: TReportInfo);
    property ReportInfo: TReportInfo read FReportInfo write FReportInfo;
  end;

  TSalesReport = class
  private
    FReportInfo: TReportInfo;
  public
    constructor Create(aReportInfo: TReportInfo);
    property ReportInfo: TReportInfo read FReportInfo write FReportInfo;
  end;

constructor TInventoryReport.Create(aReportInfo: TReportInfo);
begin
  FReportInfo := aReportInfo;
end;

constructor TSalesReport.Create(aReportInfo: TReportInfo);
begin
  FReportInfo := aReportInfo;
end;

var
  ReportInfo: TReportInfo;
  NewReportInfo: TReportInfo;
  InventoryReport: TInventoryReport;
  SalesReport: TSalesReport;

begin
  try
    ReportInfo := TReportInfo.Create;
    InventoryReport := TInventoryReport.Create(ReportInfo);
    SalesReport := TSalesReport.Create(ReportInfo);
    try
      // Do Stuff with reports

      NewReportInfo := TReportInfo.Create;
      try
        InventoryReport.ReportInfo := NewReportInfo;
        // Do stuff with report
        // But the reports now point to different ReportInfos.
        // This is Connascence of Identity
      finally
        NewReportInfo.Free;
      end;
    finally
      ReportInfo.Free;
      InventoryReport.Free;
      SalesReport.Free;
    end;
  except
```

```
    on E: Exception do
      Writeln(E.ClassName, ': ', E.Message);
  end;
end.
```

Here we have two reports: an inventory report and a sales report. The domain requires that the two reports always refer to the same instance of `TReportInfo`. However, as you can see above, in the middle of the reporting process the Inventory Report gets a new ReportInfo instance. This is fine, but the Sales Report needs to refer to this new `TReportInfo` instance, as well. In other words, if you change the reference in one report, the other report has to change to the same reference. This is called Connascence of Identity, as the two classes must both change the identity of their reference in order for the system to continue working correctly.

What to Do About Connascence?

Well, now that we have the nine Levels of Connascence defined, what should we do about the coupling in our code?

While some coupling must take place, you should endeavor to keep your connascence at the lowest level possible. That is, you should reduce the Degree of Connascence in your code. A very clean application will commonly have Connascence of Name and of Type, and will try to limit Connascence of Meaning and Position as much as possible. All other types of connascence should really be refactored out.

You should also increase the Locality of Connascence in your code. You should work to reduce the scope of all identifiers in your code. You should limit the scope of a type to as low a scope as possible. Things that belong together should be kept together and not exposed to places that they don't belong. The DRY principle – "Don't repeat yourself" – is an example of increasing locality. So is the Single Responsibility Principle.

Finally, you should prefer stability. Connascence is really just the measure of the need for change, and the less often you need to change something, the less often errors will occur as a result of tight coupling. Things that are stable will be much less likely to cause coupling errors.

Conclusion

We all agree that tight coupling is bad (at least I hope we do!). But the notion of coupling has typically been rather ill-defined. I hope this review of connascence – the idea that if something changes in one place, something else has to change somewhere else – will allow you to talk a bit more specifically about what coupling is. I also hope that the Levels of Connascence will allow you find code with a high degree of coupling and refactor those areas to lower your coupling. If you endeavor to reduce the overall level of Connascence in your code, you'll have a cleaner and easier to maintain codebase.

Constructor Injection

Okay, so in the first chapter, you saw code that injected one class into another. This reduced the coupling and made the dependency weaker. The class was injected via the constructor. You'll probably be stunned to know that this is called "Constructor Injection." In this chapter, I'll talk a bit more in depth about constructor injection.

Constructor Injection

Constructor Injection is the process of using the constructor to pass in the dependencies of a class. The dependencies are declared as parameters of the constructor. As a result, you cannot create a new instance of the class without passing in a variable of the type required by the constructor.

That last point is key – when you declare a dependency as a parameter on the constructor, you are saying "I'm sorry, folks, but if you want to create this class, you ***must*** pass in this parameter." Thus, a class is able to specify the dependencies that it requires and be guaranteed that it will get them. You can't create the class without them. If you have this code:

```
TPayrollSystem = class
private
  FBankingService: TBankingService;
public
  constructor Create(aBankingService: TBankingService);
end;

constructor TPayrollSystem.Create(aBankingService: TBankingService);
begin
  FBankingService := aBankingService;
end;
```

you can't create a `TPayrollSystem` without passing it an instance of `TBankingService`. (Well, sadly, you can pass `nil`, but we'll deal with that in a minute.) `TPayrollSystem` very clearly declares that it requires a `TBankingService`, and users of the class must supply one.

Never Accept `nil`

As I mentioned, it is unfortunate that the above class can and will take `nil` as a parameter. I say "take" because while a user of the class can pass in `nil`, the class itself doesn't have to accept `nil`. In fact, I argue that all methods should explicitly reject `nil` as a value for any reference parameter at any time, including constructors and regular methods. At no time should a parameter allowed to be `nil` without the method raising an exception. If you pass `nil` to the `TPayrollSystem` above and the class tries to use it, an access violation will occur. And access violations are bad. They should – and in this case can – be avoided.

The above code really should look something like this:

```
TPayrollSystem = class
private
  FBankingService: TBankingService;
public
  constructor Create(aBankingService: TBankingService);
end;

constructor TPayrollSystem.Create(aBankingService: TBankingService);
begin
  if aBankingService = nil then
  begin
    raise Exception.Create('What the heck do you think you are doing?  How dare you pass me a nil bank\
ing service!?!');
  end;

  FBankingService := aBankingService;
end;
```

This code will never allow the internal field to be `nil`. It will raise an exception if someone dares pass in `nil` as the value for the constructor's parameter. This is how it should be. You could accept `nil`, but then you'd have to check for it everywhere in your code, and who wants that? In the immortal words of Barney Fife, you should nip the use of `nil` in the bud by refusing to accept it at the entry point.

Checking for `nil` is boilerplate code, and the Spring4D framework provides a means for easily doing a `nil` check. Protecting against `nil` being passed as a parameter is called the "Guard Pattern," and you won't be surprised to know that Spring4D provides a record called `Guard` that has a number of static methods that allow you to check – or "guard against" – certain situations from occurring.

> The Guard Pattern actually is defined as any Boolean expression that must evaluate to True before the program execution can continue. It is usually used to ensure that certain preconditions are met before a method can continue, ensuring that the code that follows can properly execute. Checking that a reference is not `nil` is probably the most common – but not the only – use for the Guard Pattern.

In the case at hand, we are using the Guard Pattern to protect against a parameter being nil, so we can use the Guard class to simplify our code:

```
TPayrollSystem = class
private
  FBankingService: TBankingService;
public
  constructor Create(aBankingService: TBankingService);
end;

constructor TPayrollSystem.Create(aBankingService: TBankingService);
begin
  Guard.CheckNotNull(aBankingService, 'aBankingService');
  FBankingService := aBankingService;
end;
```

`Guard.CheckNotNull` takes two parameters. The first is the item to be checked, and the second is the name of the item that was checked as a string. Now, if you pass `nil` to the constructor, you'll get this error:

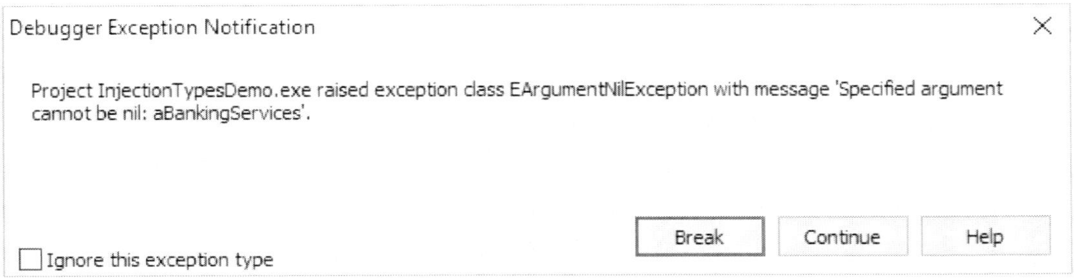

A Guard clause error

Okay, enough about passing `nil`. You should have the message by now.

When to Use Constructor Injection

You should use Constructor Injection when your class has a dependency which the class requires in order to work properly. If your class cannot work without a dependency, then inject it via the constructor. If your class needs three dependencies, then demand all three in the constructor. (In the chapter on Anti-Patterns, we'll discuss the situation where you end up with lots of dependencies in the constructor.)

Additionally, you should use Constructor Injection when the dependency in question has a lifetime longer than a single method. Dependencies passed into the constructor should be useful to the class in a general way, with its use spanning multiple methods in the class. If a dependency is used in only one spot, Method Injection (covered in a coming chapter) should be used.

Constructor Injection should be the main way that you do dependency injection. It's simple: A class needs something and thus asks for it before it can even be constructed. By using the Guard Pattern, you can use the class with confidence, knowing that the field variable storing that dependency will be a valid instance. Plus, it's really simple and clear to do. Constructor Injection should be your go-to technique for clear, decoupled code. But it shouldn't be the only tool in the toolbox. Coming up – other ways and reasons for injecting dependencies.

Property Injection

Okay, so we use Constructor Injection when we want to declare required dependencies. But what to do when a dependency isn't required? Sometimes a class has a dependency that isn't strictly required but is indeed used by the class. An example might be a document class that may or may not have a grammar checker installed. If there is one, great; the class can use it. If there isn't one, great – the class can include a default implementation as a placeholder.

The solution here is Property Injection. You add a property on your class that can be set to a valid instance of the class in question. Since the dependency is a property, you can set it as desired. If the dependency is not wanted or needed, you can leave the property as is. Your code should act like the dependency is there, so you should provide a do-nothing default implementation so that the code can still be run with or without a real dependency. (Remember, we never want anything to be `nil`, so that default implementation should be valid). Thus, if the user of the class wants to provide a working implementation, he or she can, but if not, there is a working default that will allow the containing class to still function.

> Use Property Injection when a dependency is optional and/or when a dependency can be changed after the class is instantiated. Use it when you want users of the containing class to be able to provide their own implementation of the interface in question. You should only use Property Injection when you can provide a default implementation of the interface in question. Property Injection is sometimes referred to as "Setter Injection."

Any default implementation will likely be a non-functional implementation. But it doesn't have to be. If you want to provide a working default implementation, that is fine. However, be aware that by using Property Injection and creating that class in the containing object's `constructor`, you are coupling yourself to that implementation. But don't despair; there are ways to deal with that when we start using a Container. But we aren't that far yet, hence the warning.

An example, of course, will show how things are done. Let's take a look at code that does what I described above – a document class that has an optional grammar checker.

First, we'll start with an interface:

```
type
  IGrammarChecker = interface
  ['{9CA7F68C-8A42-4B8C-AD1A-14C04CAE0901}']
    procedure CheckGrammar;
  end;
```

Now, we'll implement it twice. Once as a do-nothing default and again as a "real" grammar checker.

```
type
  TDefaultGrammarChecker = class(TInterfacedObject, IGrammarChecker)
  private
    procedure CheckGrammar;
  end;

  TRealGrammarChecker = class(TInterfacedObject, IGrammarChecker)
    procedure CheckGrammar;
  end;

procedure TDefaultGrammarChecker.CheckGrammar;
begin
  // do nothing, but we'll WriteLn just to prove we were here
  WriteLn('Do nothing');
end;

procedure TRealGrammarChecker.CheckGrammar;
begin
  WriteLn('Grammar has been checked');
end;
```

Both of the implementations do a `WriteLn`, even the "no-op" implementation. I merely wanted to makes sure that things were all working properly. Again, `TDefaultGrammarChecker` is meant to be a non-operational, default implementation that will keep us from having to check for `nil` all the time.

Now we need a class that has a property on it for the grammar checker.

```
  TDocument = class
  private
    FText: string;
    FGrammarChecker: IGrammarChecker;
    procedure SetGrammarChecker(const Value: IGrammarChecker);
  public
    constructor Create(const aText: string);
    procedure CheckGrammar;
    property Text: string read FText write FText;
    property GrammarChecker: IGrammarChecker read FGrammarChecker write SetGrammarChecker;
  end;

procedure TDocument.CheckGrammar;
begin
  FGrammarChecker.CheckGrammar;
end;

constructor TDocument.Create(const aText: string);
begin
  inherited Create;
  FText := aText;
  FGrammarChecker := TDefaultGrammarChecker.Create;
end;

procedure TDocument.SetGrammarChecker(const Value: IGrammarChecker);
begin
  Guard.CheckNotNull(Value, 'Value in TDocument.SetGrammarChecker');
  FGrammarChecker := Value;
end;
```

Here are some things to note about this code:

- Its `constructor` takes the document text as a parameter. It's then exposed as a read/write property, so you can change it if you want.
- The `constructor` also creates an instance of the default grammar checker. Note again that this creates a hard-coded dependency – one of the perils of Property Injection. But the dependency is a do-nothing default and prevents us from having constantly to check for `nil`.
- The setter for the `GrammarChecker` property contains a `Guard` call, ensuring that the internal value for `FGrammarChecker` can never be `nil`.

One further thing that you might note is that the `GrammarChecker` property could actually be a "write-only" property if you wanted it to be. That is, you could only set the value and never actually read it.

> You can create a write-only property when the value being written is only used internally and will never be called by code outside of the class. Something like the GrammarChecker might qualify as a write-only property.

Now, here's some code that exercises everything and shows Property Injection in action:

```
procedure Main;
var
  Document: TDocument;
begin
  Document := TDocument.Create('This is the document text.');
  try
    WriteLn(Document.Text);
    // Use the default, no-op grammar checker
    Document.CheckGrammar;
    // Change the dependency to use the "real" grammar checker
    Document.GrammarChecker := TRealGrammarChecker.Create;
    // Now the grammar checker is a "real" one
    Document.CheckGrammar;
    // This will -- and should -- raise an exception.
    Document.GrammarChecker := nil;
  finally
    Document.Free;
  end;
end;
```

Here are things to note about the above code: * It creates a document, taking some text as a constructor parameter. * It calls `CheckGrammar`, but the default grammar checker doesn't do anything, so it says so in the console. * But then we use Property Injection to inject a "real" grammar checker, and when we call `CheckGrammar`, the grammar gets checked "for real." * Then we try to set the grammar checker to `nil`, but that raises an exception because of the `Guard` clause.

Thus, Property Injection allows you to provide optional dependencies. It also allows you to change a dependency, if required. For instance, your document class may take texts from different languages and thus will require that the grammar checker changes as the document's language changes. Property Injection will allow for this.

Method Injection

What if the dependency that your class needs is going to be different much of the time? What if the dependency is an interface, and you have several implementations that you may want to pass in to the class? You could use Property Injection, but then you'd be setting the property all the time before calling the method that utilized the frequently-changing dependency, setting up the possibility of temporal coupling.

> Temporal Coupling is the basically the same as Connascence of Execution – the idea that the order of execution must occur in a specific way for things to work correctly.

Constructor and Property Injection are generally used when you have one dependency that isn't going to change often, so they aren't appropriate for use when your dependency may be one of many implementations.

This is where Method Injection comes in.

Method Injection allows you to inject a dependency right at the point of use, so that you can pass any implementation you want without having to worry about storing it for later use. It is often used when you pass in other information that needs special handling. For example:

```
unit uPropertyInjectionMultiple;

interface

type

  TRecipe = class
  private
    FText: string;
  public
    property Text: string read FText write FText;
  end;

  IFoodPreparer = interface
```

```
  ['{3900BE64-B0EC-4281-9D92-96B191FDE5BC}']
    procedure PrepareFood(aRecipe: TRecipe);
  end;

  TBaker = class(TInterfacedObject, IFoodPreparer)
    procedure PrepareFood(aRecipe: TRecipe);
  end;

  TShortOrderCook = class(TInterfacedObject, IFoodPreparer)
    procedure PrepareFood(aRecipe: TRecipe);
  end;

  TChef = class(TInterfacedObject, IFoodPreparer)
    procedure PrepareFood(aRecipe: TRecipe);
  end;

  TRestaurant = class
  private
    FName: string;
  public
    constructor Create(const aName: string);
    procedure PrepareFood(aRecipe: TRecipe; aPreparer: IFoodPreparer);
    property Name: string read FName;
  end;

implementation

constructor TRestaurant.Create(const aName: string);
begin
  FName := aName;
end;

procedure TRestaurant.PrepareFood(aRecipe: TRecipe; aPreparer: IFoodPreparer);
begin
  aPreparer.PrepareFood(aRecipe)
end;

procedure TBaker.PrepareFood(aRecipe: TRecipe);
begin
  Writeln('Use baking skills to do the following: ' + aRecipe.Text);
end;

procedure TShortOrderCook.PrepareFood(aRecipe: TRecipe);
begin
  Writeln('Use the grill to do the following: ' + aRecipe.Text);
end;

procedure TChef.PrepareFood(aRecipe: TRecipe);
begin
  Writeln('Use well-trained culinary skills to prepare the following: ' + aRecipe.Text);
end;

end.
```

Here, we have the notion of a recipe, which may require a different preparer depending on that recipe. Only the calling entity will know what the proper preparer type will be for a given recipe. For instance, one recipe might require a short-order cook, and another recipe might require a baker or a chef. We don't know when writing the code what kind of `IFoodPreparer` will be needed, and thus we can't really pass the dependency in the constructor and be stuck with that one implementation.

It is also clumsy to set a property every time a new or different `IFoodPreparer` is required. And setting the property in such a way induces temporal coupling (Connascence of Execution) and will suffer from thread-safety issues because it would require a lock around the code in a threaded environment.

The best solution is to just pass the `IFoodPreparer` into the method at the point of use.

Method injection should be used when the dependency could change with every use, or at least when you can't be sure which dependency will be needed at the point of use.

Here's an example of using Method Injection when the dependency needs to change every time it is used. Imagine a situation where a car-painting robot requires a new paint-gun tip after every car it paints. You might start out like this using Constructor Injection:

```
type

  IPaintGunTip = interface
    procedure SprayCar(aColor: TColor);
  end;

  TPaintGunTip = class(TInterfacedObject, IPaintGunTip)
    procedure SprayCar(aColor: TColor);
  end;

  TCarPaintingRobot = class
  private
    FPaintGunTip: IPaintGunTip;
  public
    constructor Create(aPaintGunTip: IPaintGunTip);
    procedure PaintCar(aColor: TColor);
  end;

constructor TCarPaintingRobot.Create(aPaintGunTip: IPaintGunTip);
begin
  Guard.CheckNotNull(aPaintGunTip, 'aPaintGunTip');
```

```
  FPaintGunTip := aPaintGunTip;
end;

procedure TCarPaintingRobot.PaintCar(aColor: TColor);
begin
  FPaintGunTip.SprayCar(aColor);

  // Uh oh -- what to do now?  How do we free the tip?
  // And even if we could, what then?
  // How would we get a new one?

end;

procedure TPaintGunTip.SprayCar(aColor: TColor);
begin
  Writeln('Spray the car with ', ColorToString(aColor));
end;
```

> When implementing a method using Method Injection, you *must* include a Guard Clause. The dependency will be immediately used, and, of course, if you try to use it when it is `nil`, you'll get an immediate Access Violation. This should obviously be avoided.

Here, when we paint the car, we have to get a new paint gun tip. But how? When we paint the car, the tip is no good anymore, but it's an interface, and we have no way to manually free it, and even if we did, what would we do the next time we need to paint a car? We don't know what kind of tip is needed for a given car, and if we have properly separated our concerns, we don't even know anything about creating a new tip. What to do? Well, use method injection instead:

```
type

  IPaintGunTip = interface
    procedure SprayCar(aColor: TColor);
  end;

  TPaintGunTip = class(TInterfacedObject, IPaintGunTip)
    procedure SprayCar(aColor: TColor);
  end;

  TCarPaintingRobot = class
  public
    procedure PaintCar(aColor: TColor; aPaintGunTip: IPaintGunTip);
  end;

procedure TCarPaintingRobot.PaintCar(aColor: TColor; aPaintGunTip: IPaintGunTip);
```

```
begin
  aPaintGunTip.SprayCar(aColor);
end;

procedure TPaintGunTip.SprayCar(aColor: TColor);
begin
  WriteLn('Spray the car with ', ColorToString(aColor));
end;
```

Now, when we pass the dependency directly to the method, the interface goes out of scope when we are done painting and the paint gun tip is destroyed. In addition, the next time a car needs to be painted, the consumer will pass in a new tip, which will be freed upon use. Method Injection to the rescue!

Thus Method Injection is useful in two scenarios: when the implementation of a dependency will vary and when the dependency needs to be renewed after each use. In both cases, it is up to the caller to decide what implementation to pass to the method.

The Dependency Injection Container

Up to this point I've only made glancing reference to the notion of a Dependency Injection Container. I've done that on purpose for a couple of reasons. First, I wanted to make sure that you understood Dependency Injection before we talked about the Dependency Injection Container. As I noted at the start, Dependency Injection and using a Dependency Injection Container are two very different things. You can do Dependency Injection without ever touching a Dependency Injection Container. That's what we've been doing so far. Second, there is a lot of confusion about what a Container is, how to use it, where to use it and when to use it. I wanted to delay answering those questions as long as possible so that you get the idea of Dependency Injection without the potential confusion of what the Container is and does.

But the time has come, and so now we'll take a look at the famous – or infamous – Dependency Injection Container.

What is a Dependency Injection Container?

Answering the question "What is a Dependency Injection Container?" has been a difficult one since the idea originated. Many people have differing views of how to answer that question. I obviously have my own definition, but before I get to that, I'll talk first about what a Container is *not*.

A Container is *not* merely a replacement for a call to `Create`. While a large part of what it does is create objects, it is not quite that simple. You certainly should not merely replace all of your constructor calls with calls to the Container (or – shudder – the `ServiceLocator`), and you certainly should not use it to create local method variables. For example, the following code should be considered an anti-pattern:

```
procedure TWidgetManager.ProcessWidget(aWidget: TWidget);
var
  WidgetProcessor: IWidgetProcessor;
begin
  WidgetProcessor := ServiceLocator.GetService<IWidgetProcessor>;
  WidgetProcessor.ProcessWidget(aWidget);
end;
```

Here, we have merely replaced a call to `TWidgetProcessor.Create` with a call to the given Container. This should be steadfastly avoided. Often, this is referred to as the `ServiceLocator` pattern (or anti-pattern, as I believe) because of the tendency to use a `ServiceLocator` class to access the Container. I'll discuss the `ServiceLocator` anti-pattern in a later chapter.

A Container is not merely a dictionary of class implementations and services. If you view it that way, it becomes a big bucket of global variables, and everyone agrees that global variables are undesirable. Such a view is similar to the "replacement for `Create`" view in that if you hold it, you'll see the Container as nothing more than "a place to get objects," when in fact, it is more than that.

What is the Container?

A Container ***is*** a means of composing your application's object graph. It manages the creation of dependencies along with their lifetimes. A Container creates and manages dependencies as needed, or rather even before they are needed. Think of your classes as empty balloons in a box. When your application starts up, you press a button and all of the balloons are filled with air and ready to be used. As we'll see – and to continue the metaphor – you can instruct the Container in the correct way to fill the balloons and the proper amount of air to inflate each one. You can delay the inflation of balloons, you can pick which kind of balloons are inflated, and you can choose what balloons get composed together in bunches. The Container gives you total control over your balloons, if you will. Thus it becomes more than a glorified instance of the factory pattern and instead it is a powerful, flexible – yes – Container for your objects.

Why is a Container Needed?

Before I answer that question, I want to point out that a Dependency Injection Container is ***not*** always needed. Sometimes, good old Constructor, Property, and Method Injection are enough, and a Container is overkill. Depending on how complex your object graph is, you may be able to get away with creating your own objects manually, or simply using factories to create your classes.

There's no shame in doing what Mark Seamann has referred to as "Pure DI." In fact, Pure DI can be quite illuminating. If you do it correctly, you will eventually arrive at the Composition Root (The Composition Root will be discussed a bit further below) of your application, with a very clear view of how your Object Graph is constructed. What objects your application requires and how they are created will be plain to see.

Pure DI is also strongly typed. Those Constructor Injection parameters all have a type attached to them, and if the typing isn't right, the compiler is going to complain. Compile-time feedback is immediate and thus will allow us to avoid bugs that can result when we depend on run-time feeback.

Given that you don't, strictly speaking "need" a DI Container, you will very likely find yourself wanting to use one. You will probably end up wanting a Container because an application of any consequence will have a rather extensive object graph at the Composition Root. Creating all those objects can get cumbersome. A Container can unencumber you from having to create everything manually.

Perhaps this question has already occurred to you: "If I keep asking for my dependencies and never create them, where the heck ***do*** they get created?" Well, that is a very good question. The answer is what you've now likely surmised – they are all created in the Container. The Container manages their creation and their lifetime. It can, with but a single call (we'll talk about that below), do everything and manage everything you need for your whole application.

Where to Use the Container

Perhaps this is another question you've had: "If I continue to 'push back' the creation of my objects via Dependency Injection, won't all of my create calls end up in the

DPR file? That's a lot of Create calls!" Well, you wonder that because that is exactly what will happen. If you use Dependency Injection in a dedicated manner – and you should – your constructors will all end up at what is called the "Composition Root" of your application. In a Delphi application, this is the main block of the DPR file – the place where every Delphi application starts. And it is there that you should use the Container. It is there that you should make a single call to the Container to `Resolve` the entire object graph for your application.

You should delay the connecting of your classes together – your Object Composition – as long as possible. The longer you delay it, the more flexible you can be and the more freedom you have in deciding how to do it. Doing this – delaying things – is what makes the use of a DI Container possible. You can delay things to a single point at the very root of your application and then let the DI Container do the composing for you.

When to Use the Container

The question of when to use the Container has two answers.

The first is "all the time." You should always use Dependency Injection and a Dependency Injection Container in any application of consequence that you build. It should be the normal, accepted, everyday way that you build applications. It should be as much a part of your toolbox as integers and classes and lists.

I alluded to the second answer above: you should use the Container once and only once at the composite root of your application. At this point you are likely wondering how that is possible – there are too many classes! – but I assure you it can and should be done. I'll discuss this in the coming chapters.

But of course, the use of a Dependency Injection Container has costs associated with it, and naturally you should consider those costs before making the decision to use one. The main cost of using a DI Container is the time one needs to spend to learn it. (Indeed, you have to buy and read a whole book on the subject!) Planning and designing for the use of a DI Container doesn't come free. In addition, there is the overhead of adding a non-trivial framework to your application.

Another cost involved with using a DI Container is the loss of compile-time type checking. This is non-trivial. The compiler is your first line of defense against errors, and if you use plain old Dependency Injection, the compiler will most often tell you if you've made a mistake. However, with a DI Container, you lose that. Because your object graph is created and bound at run-time, you'll get runtime errors if you make a mistake. If you forget to register an implementation for a given interface, you won't know that until you try to get that missing implementation at run-time. This is not a small cost. You will definitely need to take care to ensure that your code is properly composed to avoid this.

However, if one uses a DI Container properly, the benefits should far outweigh the costs. Those benefits are what I'll talk about in the rest of this book.

Capabilities and Functionality

What Container to Use?

You should use a container that you create for yourself. The Spring for Delphi framework provides a singleton `GlobalContainer`, but use of it should be avoided given that it is, well, a global variable. Instead, you should create your own instance of a container and use that for registering and resolving your implementations.

Simple Object Registration

Registering a class with the Container is as easy as can be:

```
MyContainer.RegisterType<TMyClass>;
```

That's it. Now your Container knows about `TMyClass` and can retrieve an instance of `TMyClass` whenever it needs to. If another class has `TMyClass` as a dependency, the Container will know how to get it automatically. So, for instance, say you register another class that has `TMyClass` injected in the constructor:

```
type
  TAnotherClasss = class
    constructor Create(aMyClass: TMyClass);
  end;

  ....

  MyContainer.RegisterType<TAnotherClass>
```

Then if you reference `TAnotherClass`, the Container will simply provide you with an instance of `TMyClass` for your constructor. No need for you to do anything. The Container will see your need, find the most specific constructor that has all the dependencies it knows about, and create the class for you. In fact, it will do all this before you even ask for it. This is all part of "creating your object graph" for you. This is a simple example of how the Container is more than just a bag of classes waiting to be used.

Interface Implementation

I mentioned previously that you should always code against an abstraction – usually an interface – and not an implementation. Well, the Container makes that really easy to do. By registering an interface and an implementation together, you can tell the Container that a given class implements an interface, and then, as above, when you need an implementation for a given interface, the Container will supply it:

```
MyContainer.RegisterType<ILogger, TLogger>;
```

> Astute readers might note that this is a different syntax for registering classes against interfaces from my previous books. Previously, you registered them using the `Implements` method, but the above way to do the registration is now the preferred method for associating a class and an interface.

The code above basically says "Register the `ILogger` interface and use the `TLogger` implementation for it." In this way, you can use interfaces when doing Dependency Injection, and the Container will support you in your quest to always code against abstractions.

Multiple Implementations per Interface

But what if you have more than one class that implements the same interface? Well, you can register classes by name:

```
MyContainer.RegisterType<ILogger, TFileLogger>('file');
MyContainer.RegisterType<ILogger, TConsoleLogger('console'),
MyContainer.RegisterType<ILogger, TDatabaseLogger('database');
```

Given the above, you can choose your desired implementation from the three registrations based on the name.

Lifetime Management

One of the key features of the Container is the ability to manage the lifetime of objects that it supplies to you. In Delphi, of course, you are responsible for ensuring the proper disposal of the memory allocated by the construction of an object. If you have the Container allocate the object for you, then you can instruct the Container on how to manage the lifetime of that object.

In Delphi, you are generally responsible for freeing any object that you create. In the VCL, there is the exception that any VCL object that is owned by another VCL object will be freed by the owning object. In addition, if your object is referenced as an interface, the compiler will do reference counting and automatically free your object when the reference goes completely out of scope and the reference count goes to zero.

But if you turn the responsibility of creating your object graph over to the Dependency Injection Container, then the Container takes on the task of managing the lifetime of the objects it creates. This means you don't have to do it because the Container is responsible for an object's lifetime. It also means that you need to let the Container know how you'd like to have the lifetime of your objects managed. You can do this with calls to the Container as defined by the table below:

Type	Description
AsTransient	This is the default. It creates one instance per request, and that request lives as long as the variable is in scope. In other words, a new instance is created for every request.
AsSingleton	Creates a single instance of the class and returns that instance for every request made for that class. That single class is used for all references to the object.
AsSingeltonPerThread	Same as `AsSingleton`, but creates an instance on a per thread basis.
AsPooled	Creates a pool of objects of a user-configurable size and then hands out instances from that pool.

By now you might have noticed that the Spring4D Container uses the fluent interface. A look into the source code shows that each call to the Container always returns an instance of `TRegistration<T>`, enabling you to chain calls to the Container together. `TRegistration<T>` is a class that manages all the functionality of the Container, while at the same time allowing you to create a single statement that defines an entire registration of a class. So, for instance, you can have statements like the following:

```
  MyContainer.RegisterType<IFirearm, TRifle>('rifle').AsSingleton.InjectProperty('MetalSight', 'sight'\
).InjectField('Clip');
```

which will register a class against an interface and declare it to be a singleton, as well as inject a property value and a field value. It's a powerful and easy to read way to declare dependencies. Fluent interfaces often read like sentences.

If you want to have your reference be a singleton – that is, one instance for all calls to the given registration – then declare it as follows:

```
MyContainer.RegisterType<IWeapon, TSword>.AsSingleton;
```

That will ensure that whenever you ask for an `IWeapon`, you will be given back the same exact instance of `TSword` for all requests.

`AsSingletonPerThread` does what its name implies – it provides the same instance to each request within a given thread. There might be multiple instances of the implementation, but each thread will always get its own instance.

`AsTransient` is the default behavior. `AsTransient` will create a new instance for each request made. Assuming that you are using an interface reference, that transient instance will live as long as the interface remains in scope (i.e., as long as its reference count is greater than zero, presuming you are using "normal" reference counting). Transient is the least efficient of the lifetime management choices, because it can cause the Container to create a large number of classes that live a long time.

`AsPooled` will create a pool of instances for use upon request. You can determine the minimum and maximum number of items in the pool. When an item is resolved by the Container, it will be retrieved from the pool of items. All the items in the pool are created when the Container is built, and thus all are available when the program begins. Use pooling when creation is expensive and you want to pay that cost up front or when you have a limited number of resources and want to ensure that no more instances of the class representing the resource are created than there are resources. Pooled items are never shared, so this may be a reason to choose it, as well.

DelegateTo

Sometimes, the constructor of your class might not perfectly cooperate with the Container and be a resolvable dependency. Consider the following class:

```
type
  IWindowsUser = interface
  ['{432973CE-CDDF-45CC-9BA0-EC089F23EAF4}']
    function GetUserName: string;
    property UserName: string read GetUserName;
  end;

  TWindowsUser = class(TInterfacedObject, IWindowsUser)
  private
    FUserName: string;
    function GetUserName: string;
  public
    constructor Create(const aUserName: string);
    property Username: string read GetUsername;
  end;
```

First, we declare an interface, `IWindowsUser`, that represents a user name on a Windows system. We also provide an implementing class that takes a `string` as its parameter to the constructor. We'd like this interface implemented inside of our Container, so we declare the following:

```
MyContainer.RegisterType<IWindowsUser, TWindowsUser>.DelegateTo(function: TWindowsUser
                                         begin
                                           Result := TWindowsUser.Create(GetLocalUserName);
                                         end)
```

Next, we register `TWindowsUser` as implementing the `IWindowsUser` interface. Remember, in order for a class to have its constructor parameters automatically resolved, you need to register that class with the Container. However, here there is a hitch: the constructor takes a `string` as a parameter – a string that changes every time a new user logs on to Windows. Thus, it's not clear how the Container should go about creating an instance of `TWindowsUser`. Therefore, we define for the Container exactly how we want `TWindowsUser` constructed for us via a call to `DelegateTo`. This method takes an anonymous function that returns a `TWindowsUser`, giving you the opportunity to tell the Container how to create a `TWindowsUser`.

As a side note, `GetLocalUserName` is declared as follows:

```
function GetLocalUserName: string;
var
  aLength: DWORD;
  aUserName: array [0 .. Max_Path - 1] of Char;
begin
  aLength := Max_Path;
  if not GetUserName(aUserName, aLength) then
  begin
    raise Exception.CreateFmt('Win32 Error %d: %s', [GetLastError, SysErrorMessage(GetLastError)]);
  end;
  Result := string(aUserName);
end;
```

Use `DelegateTo` when the Container otherwise won't know how to create an instance of a class. This might happen because the constructor's parameters are not resolvable by the Container, or because the information needed by the constructor is dependent on external information that can't be stored in the Container.

There are some caveats to using `DelegateTo`. You should be very careful to limit the use of `DelegateTo` and find ways for the Container to solve this problem. Otherwise, you could very easily end up with many calls to `DelegateTo` which themselves merely call the Container. This really becomes just another form of Pure DI, but with the overhead of the container included.

Conclusion

That's the basics of the Container. A DI Container is an extremely useful tool. It can allow you to, in a single spot with a single line of code, compose your entire object graph. Thus, your application can be made up of many loosely coupled classes that ask for their dependencies and that know nothing of the Container itself. Later, I'll cover some more advanced topics that super-charge what you can do with the Container, but for now you should have enough tools to take a look at a basic example that illustrates how the Container works and how it should be used. That's what I'll do in the next chapter.

A Step-by-Step Example

So far we've looked at simple examples that show off the Container's specific capabilities. But how does all of this really work? What are we really talking about here? In this chapter, we'll take a look at an example that starts out "normal" – how things are traditionally done – and then move on to show how it can be refactored to be clean and decoupled, as well as easy to test and maintain by taking advantage of the power of a Dependency Injection Container.

The Beginning

> The code for this chapter can be found at: http://bit.ly/diidcode

First, we'll start off at the root of our demo application, the call to `DoOrderProcessing`, which is called in the project's DPR file:

```
procedure DoOrderProcessing;
var
  Order: TOrder;
  OrderProcessor: TOrderProcessor;
begin
  Order := TOrder.Create;
  try
    OrderProcessor := TOrderProcessor.Create;
    try
      if OrderProcessor.ProcessOrder(Order) then
      begin
        WriteLn('Order successfully processed....');
      end;
    finally
      OrderProcessor.Free;
    end;
  finally
    Order.Free;
  end;
end;
```

Here, we see some pretty typical code. An order is created and then processed by an order processor. Once the processing is done, the processor is freed. Very simple, basic code. You probably have done something like this a million times.

What does `TOrderProcessor` look like?

```
type
  TOrderProcessor = class
  private
    FOrderValidator: TOrderValidator;
    FOrderEntry: TOrderEntry;
  public
    constructor Create;
    destructor Destroy; override;
    function ProcessOrder(aOrder: TOrder): Boolean;
  end;

constructor TOrderProcessor.Create;
begin
  FOrderValidator := TOrderValidator.Create;
  FOrderEntry := TOrderEntry.Create;
end;

destructor TOrderProcessor.Destroy;
begin
  FOrderValidator.Free;
  FOrderEntry.Free;
  inherited;
end;

function TOrderProcessor.ProcessOrder(aOrder: TOrder): Boolean;
var
  OrderIsValid: Boolean;
begin
  Result := False;
  OrderIsValid := FOrderValidator.ValidateOrder(aOrder);
  if OrderIsValid then
  begin
    Result := FOrderEntry.EnterOrderIntoDatabase(aOrder);
  end;
  WriteLn('Order has been processed....');
end;
```

Here are some things to note about the declaration and implementation of `TOrderProcessor`:

- The constructor is parameter-less. As a result, the two dependencies, `TOrderValidator` and `TOrderEntry`, are hard-coded via their constructor calls in the constructor of `TOrderProcessor`. We have tightly coupled ourselves to the given implementations of those two classes.

- Right away that makes this class difficult to test because we cannot replace those two dependencies with fakes.
- As is normal, we have to manage the lifetime of the dependencies manually, resulting in a destructor for the class.

Introducing Constructor Injection

Let's take some steps to make things better. First, we'll use dependency injection to inject `TOrderProcessor`'s dependencies – specifically some Constructor Injection:

```
type
  TOrderProcessor = class
  private
    FOrderValidator: TOrderValidator;
    FOrderEntry: TOrderEntry;
  public
    constructor Create(aOrderValidator: TOrderValidator; aOrderEntry: TOrderEntry);
    function ProcessOrder(aOrder: TOrder): Boolean;
  end;

constructor TOrderProcessor.Create(aOrderValidator: TOrderValidator; aOrderEntry: TOrderEntry);
begin
  FOrderValidator := aOrderValidator;
  FOrderEntry := aOrderEntry;
end;

function TOrderProcessor.ProcessOrder(aOrder: TOrder): Boolean;
var
  OrderIsValid: Boolean;
begin
  Result := False;
  OrderIsValid := FOrderValidator.ValidateOrder(aOrder);
  if OrderIsValid then
  begin
    Result := FOrderEntry.EnterOrderIntoDatabase(aOrder);
  end;
  WriteLn('Order has been processed....');
end;
```

Note that we are no longer responsible for the lifetime of the dependencies within the function – the caller is – and so the destructor has gone.

This, of course, changes our `DoOrderProcessing` procedure a bit, as we've "pushed back" the creation to closer to the base of the application:

```
procedure DoOrderProcessing;
var
  Order: TOrder;
  OrderProcessor: TOrderProcessor;
  OrderValidator: TOrderValidator;
  OrderEntry: TOrderEntry;
begin
  Order := TOrder.Create;
  try
    OrderValidator := TOrderValidator.Create;
    OrderEntry := TOrderEntry.Create;
    OrderProcessor := TOrderProcessor.Create(OrderValidator, OrderEntry);
    try
      if OrderProcessor.ProcessOrder(Order) then
      begin
        WriteLn('Order successfully processed....');
      end;
    finally
      OrderProcessor.Free;
      OrderValidator.Free;
      OrderEntry.Free;
    end;
  finally
    Order.Free;
  end;
end;
```

Here, we create the order validator and the order entry classes in the "root" of the application. (`DoOrderProcessing` is what we call in the `DPR` file). Already by this simple change we've made `TOrderProcessor` a bit more flexible. While we still couple ourselves to the specific implementations, `TOrderProcessor` itself is no longer tied specifically to any given instance of `TOrderValidator` and `TOrderEntry`. It can accept a fake of that class, or any descendent of the respective classes. It's not much, but it's something.

Coding to an Interface

How do we loosen this coupling even further? We introduce interfaces, of course. Remember, we always want to code to an interface, not an implementation. So far we've been coding to an implementation, and you can see the limitations that this is causing – we're tied to those implementations. Let's untie ourselves.

First, we'll declare some interfaces:

```
  IOrderValidator = interface
  ['{CF8834A3-F815-4F6B-A177-7AB801BEC95E}']
    function ValidateOrder(aOrder: TOrder): Boolean;
  end;

  IOrderEntry = interface
  ['{406EA68D-0733-429E-9E48-73BC660B1C72}']
    function EnterOrderIntoDatabase(aOrder: TOrder): Boolean;
  end;

  IOrderProcessor = interface
  ['{C690B9D5-8C26-4DFE-AD27-2D7A4610ACBC}']
    function ProcessOrder(aOrder: TOrder): Boolean;
  end;
```

Once these have been declared, we can code against them instead of against implementations:

```
type
  TOrderProcessor = class(TInterfacedObject, IOrderProcessor)
  private
    FOrderValidator: IOrderValidator;
    FOrderEntry: IOrderEntry;
  public
    constructor Create(aOrderValidator: IOrderValidator; aOrderEntry: IOrderEntry);
    function ProcessOrder(aOrder: TOrder): Boolean;
  end;

constructor TOrderProcessor.Create(aOrderValidator: IOrderValidator; aOrderEntry: IOrderEntry);
begin
  FOrderValidator := aOrderValidator;
  FOrderEntry := aOrderEntry;
end;

function TOrderProcessor.ProcessOrder(aOrder: TOrder): Boolean;
var
  OrderIsValid: Boolean;
begin
  Result := False;
  OrderIsValid := FOrderValidator.ValidateOrder(aOrder);
  if OrderIsValid then
  begin
    Result := FOrderEntry.EnterOrderIntoDatabase(aOrder);
  end;
  WriteLn('Order has been processed....');
end;
```

First, we've changed all the references to the order validator and the order entry classes to be interfaces instead of class types. This means that now we really can pass any implementation – including fakes for testing purposes – to `TOrderProcessor`. Since we are coding against an interface, we can also remove the calls to `Free`. Here's what the call to `DoOrderProcessing` looks like now:

```
procedure DoOrderProcessing;
var
  Order: TOrder;
  OrderProcessor: IOrderProcessor;
  OrderValidator: IOrderValidator;
  OrderEntry: IOrderEntry;
begin
  OrderValidator := TOrderValidator.Create;
  OrderEntry := TOrderEntry.Create;

  Order := TOrder.Create;
  try
    OrderProcessor := TOrderProcessor.Create(OrderValidator, OrderEntry);
    if OrderProcessor.ProcessOrder(Order) then
    begin
      WriteLn('Order successfully processed....');
    end;
  finally
    Order.Free;
  end;
end;
```

This is already a lot simpler. We are still hard-coded to the specific implementations of `TOrderValidator` and `TOrderEntry`, but we are another step removed from that coupling because their references are interfaces. The code is already looking a lot cleaner as a result.

Those two `Create` calls can be "pushed back" even farther – let's put them right in the composition root so that `DoOrderProcessor` doesn't require the tight-coupling to them. Here's the new `DoOrderProcessing`:

```
procedure DoOrderProcessing(aOrderValidator: IOrderValidator; aOrderEntry: IOrderEntry);
var
  Order: TOrder;
  OrderProcessor: IOrderProcessor;
begin
  Order := TOrder.Create;
  try
    OrderProcessor := TOrderProcessor.Create(aOrderValidator, aOrderEntry);
    if OrderProcessor.ProcessOrder(Order) then
    begin
      WriteLn('Order successfully processed....');
    end;
  finally
    Order.Free;
  end;
end;
```

and here's the code in the DPR file that now calls it:

```
var
  OrderValidator: IOrderValidator;
  OrderEntry: IOrderEntry;
begin
  try
    OrderValidator := TOrderValidator.Create;
    OrderEntry := TOrderEntry.Create;
    DoOrderProcessing(OrderValidator, OrderEntry);
    ReadLn;
  except
    on E: Exception do
      WriteLn(E.ClassName, ': ', E.Message);
  end;
end.
```

At this point, we've carried Dependency Injection as far as we can. We've pushed the creation of our objects all the way to the Composite Root of our application – in this case, the main block of the DPR file in Delphi. Here we create all of our dependencies right at the very beginning of the DPR file. We can't push things any farther back than that.

Now, that's all great and everything – all of our dependency creation is centralized at the root of the application – but this can lead to a big problem. If our application got much more complicated and we kept following this pattern, we'd have a huge stack of things being created in the DPR file. This would be fine, but it could get really clumsy really fast. Clumsy is not a word I'd like to describe my code. Oh, if only there were a way to manage all that creation!

Enter the Container

Of course, there is a way to manage all that creation – the Dependency Injection Container. We can take all that creating of classes that would pile up and put it all in the Container. Let's do that now.

Let's create a new unit and put all the registration there. That way, everything is centralized but neatly tucked out of the way. We'll call the unit `uRegistration.pas` and make it look like this:

```
unit uRegistration;

interface

procedure RegisterClassesAndInterfaces;

implementation

uses
      Spring.Container
    , uOrderEntry
    , uOrderValidator
    , uOrderProcessor
    ;

procedure RegisterClassesAndInterfaces(aContainer: TContainer);
begin
  aContainer.RegisterType<IOrderProcessor, TOrderProcessor>.AsSingleton;
  aContainer.RegisterType<IOrderValidator, TOrderValidator>.AsSingleton;
  aContainer.RegisterType<IOrderEntry, TOrderEntry>.AsSingleton;
  aContainer.Build;
end;

end.
```

What we've done here is pretty straight-forward. First, we've registered the `TOrder-Processor` type with the container. This lets the Container know about the class and, as we'll see, lets the Container resolve all of its dependencies automagically. In addition, we register the two classes to which we hold dependencies as implementing specific implementations. This will cause the container to resolve references to the interfaces using the concrete classes registered against them. The Container, when asked for an instance of `IOrderValidator`, will be able to supply a valid instance of `TOrderValidator` to implement it. Pretty cool. Finally, since all the classes can be singletons – they will always be asked to do the same exact thing – we register them with the lifetime management call of `AsSingleton`.

And now that we've registered these classes and interfaces, all kind of cool things happen. The first one is that the DPR file becomes really simple. The heart of the DPR ends up looking like this:

```
var
  Container: TContainer;
begin
  try
    Container := TContainer.Create;
    try
      RegisterClassesAndInterfaces(Container);
      DoOrderProcessing;
      ReadLn;
    finally
      Container.Free;
    end;
  except
    on E: Exception do
      Writeln(E.ClassName, ': ', E.Message);
  end;
end.
```

There are a couple of things to notice in this code:

- If you've downloaded and run the demo application for this chapter, you'll note that the code all runs as expected. At first glance, that might be a surprise. But of course, all will be explained.
- The variables for the two dependencies have disappeared – we don't need them anymore as we shall see.
- The parameters on `DoOrderProcessing` have disappeared, as well. We don't need them either.
- Nothing is getting created in code. That's a bit mysterious. But again, all will be explained.
- There is a call to `Container.Build`. This call is required to let the Container know to build the object graph. That's all you need to get the Container to do its magic. You should make this call once and only once at the very root of the application, as we've done here. Calling it more than once will merely cause the process to run twice and waste CPU cycles.

The really cool stuff happens within the call to `DoOrderProcessing`. Here it is in its current incarnation:

```
procedure DoOrderProcessing(aContainer: TContainer);
var
  Order: TOrder;
  OrderProcessor: IOrderProcessor;
begin
  Order := TOrder.Create;
  try
    OrderProcessor := aContainer.Resolve<IOrderProcessor>;
    if OrderProcessor.ProcessOrder(Order) then
    begin
      WriteLn('Order successfully processed....');
    end;
  finally
    Order.Free;
  end;
end;
```

Notice, again, that the parameters are gone. Then notice that the reference to `OrderProcessor` is satisfied by a single call to `aContainer.Resolve`. This single call does quite a few things. First, you'll notice that it completely instantiates an implementation of `IOrderProcessor` – in this case, an instance of `TOrderProcessor`. And this is where the "magic" happens that makes the Container more than just a factory.

Remember the declaration of TOrderProcessor?

```
  TOrderProcessor = class(TInterfacedObject, IOrderProcessor)
  private
    FOrderValidator: IOrderValidator;
    FOrderEntry: IOrderEntry;
  public
    constructor Create(aOrderValidator: IOrderValidator; aOrderEntry: IOrderEntry);
    function ProcessOrder(aOrder: TOrder): Boolean;
  end;
```

As you can see, the `constructor` takes two dependencies. So all this code runs, and nowhere do we create instances to attach to those two interface parameters. What is going on here?

What is going on is that the Container is smart enough to know what to do. Since you've registered implementations for both of those interfaces, the Container can see what you've registered and create an instance of `TOrderProcessor` by properly instantiating its constructor parameters. It's like the Container says to itself:

"Okay. I've been asked to create an implementation for `IOrderProcessor`. I see that I have `TOrderProcessor` registered as implementing `IOrderProcessor`. So, I need to create an instance of `TOrderProcessor`. Hey, look, it has a constructor! That's great, but, uh oh, it's got two dependencies that I need to resolve. The first one is `IOrderValidator`. Hey, I have a class registered for that interface! And I have one for `IOrderEntry` as well! What a relief! This means that I can create instances of those classes for the interfaces, pass those two implementations to the constructor of `TOrderProcessor`, and then return that as an implementation of `IOrderProcessor`. And then I'm done!"

All of that happens "automagically" inside the Container. Boy, that Container sure is smart, isn't it?

As a result of those smarts, we've been able to do a few things:

- Drastically reduce the amount of code we have to write. Because the container does all the creation, we don't have any calls to `Create`. The less code we have to write, the less code we have to maintain. That's a win.
- Make our code very loosely coupled. Note that all of the classes stand alone, each in their own units. We can put the interfaces into their own unit, and the only place that things come together is in the unit that registers everything with the container, and even there the relationship is merely between an interface and the implementation. That's pretty thin and thus results in loose coupling. Put another way, we only have Connascence of Name to worry about.
- Testing gets to be really easy because each class stands alone and clearly declares its dependencies. Clearly declared dependencies means that you can easily substitute fakes for those dependencies, making the classes easily testable.

By the way, if you register a class that has more than one constructor, the container will look at each one and find the most specific one that it can resolve. That is, if you have a constructor with one resolvable dependency as well as one with two resolvable dependencies, then the container will use the second one. However, I recommend that your class have just one constructor that declares all the dependencies in the class.

Conclusion

And that is how the Container can build an entire object graph while only making one `Resolve` call to the Container. Doing so results in some really sweet code. By using the Container to do all of our work, we save ourselves from writing a lot of plumbing code like creating and destroying objects, allowing us to focus on writing business logic. And as I've beaten into you now, your code will be loosely coupled and thus easy to maintain and test.
â€ƒ

Advanced Container Use

So far, I've shown you the basics of Dependency Injection, including Constructor Injection, Property (or Setter) Injection, and Method Injection. I've taken a look at the basics of how the Dependency Injection container works, and shown you a basic example of the Container doing its "magic." Now it is time to take a look at some advanced things that the container can do to make your code even more powerful.

Multiple Implementations at Runtime

As I mentioned before, you can register multiple implementations against a single interface. In this section, we'll take a look at that.

Who doesn't love fruit? Well, fruit has to be grown somewhere, and then once grown, that fruit has to be picked. But there are many different ways to pick fruit. So if we want to model the picking of fruit, it makes sense to declare an interface:

```
type
  IFruitPicker = interface
  ['{DD861C60-D9A0-411C-8448-2E3B798026DB}']
    procedure PickFruit;
  end;
```

Now that we have an interface to program against, we can pick fruit any way we like. Here are three implementations:

```
type
  THumanFruitPicker = class(TInterfacedObject, IFruitPicker)
    procedure PickFruit;
  end;

  TMechanicalFruitPicker = class(TInterfacedObject, IFruitPicker)
    procedure PickFruit;
  end;

  TAndroidFruitPicker = class(TInterfacedObject, IFruitPicker)
    procedure PickFruit;
  end;

procedure THumanFruitPicker.PickFruit;
begin
  WriteLn('Carefully hand-pick the fruit.....');
end;

procedure TMechanicalFruitPicker.PickFruit;
begin
  WriteLn('Pick the fruit with a mechanical device....');
end;

procedure TAndroidFruitPicker.PickFruit;
begin
  WriteLn('Pick the fruit with android-like robots....');
end;

end.
```

We can now have humans, machines, and android robots pick the fruit. How can we register all of these fruit-picking methods with the container and choose one to pick the fruit? Well, as follows:

```
procedure RegisterFruitPickers(aContainer: TContainer);
begin
  aContainer.RegisterType<IFruitPicker, THumanFruitPicker>('human').AsDefault;
  aContainer.RegisterType<IFruitPicker, TMechanicalFruitPicker>('mechanical');
  aContainer.RegisterType<IFruitPicker, TAndroidFruitPicker>('android');
end;
```

Notice that each of the three registrations includes a unique string that identifies the registration. That way, we can choose the implementation we want by name at runtime. Notice, too, that the `THumanFruitPicker` has been declared with the `AsDefault` method. That means that `THumanFruitPicker` will be the one used if a request is made for an `IFruitPicker` without specifying a name.

Here is the DPR file that allows you to choose which fruit picker to use:

```
type
  TPickerType = (human, mechanical, android);

var
  Name: string;
  Selection: integer;
  FruitPicker: IFruitPicker;
  Container: TContainer;
begin
  try
    Container := TContainer.Create;
    try
      RegisterFruitPickers(Container);

      WriteLn('Enter in the fruit picker to use: ');
      WriteLn('Pick 1 for a human, 2 for a machine, and 3 for an android robot.');
      ReadLn(Selection);

      Name := GetEnumName(TypeInfo(TPickerType), Selection - 1);
      FruitPicker := Container.Resolve<IFruitPicker>(Name);
      FruitPicker.PickFruit;
    finally
      Container.Free;
    end;
  except
    on E: Exception do
      WriteLn (E.ClassName, ': ', E.Message);
  end;
  ReadLn;
end.
```

Here we declare a simple enumeration that defines the three fruit pickers. We then allow you to choose a number for the fruit picker you want and use a little type info (from the `TypInfo.pas` unit) to get a string that we then use to resolve the `IFruitPicker` interface with the implementation that we want.

Running the application and selecting "2", the machine picker, gets the following result in the console:

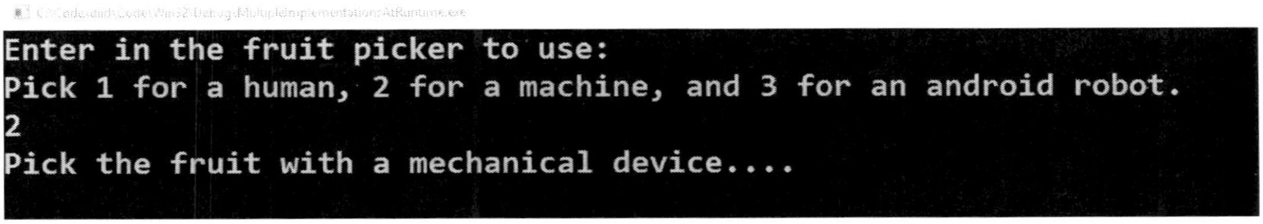

Results of picking the machine fruit picker at runtime

Thus, you can register multiple implementations for a given interface and choose whichever one you want whenever you want.

Lazy Initialization

When you call `Container.Build`, the Container will build the entire object graph all at once. This is fine – your application should be at the ready to run things when they are needed. However, sometimes a given implementation may be costly to create, or maybe it's an implementation that is unlikely to be used during the normal running of your application. In that case, you may want to do "lazy" initialization of the implementation. Lazy initialization means that the given object's construction is delayed until it is actually requested. This way, you can perhaps save some resources that don't need to be allocated right away, or prevent those resources from being allocated at all if they are rarely used.

The Spring4D Framework provides a means for you to do lazy initialization via the `Lazy<T>` record. You can declare your type as `Lazy`, and the framework won't create the given type until it is asked for.

I think an example is in order. Database connections often take time to create and often you want to create them only when needed. Let's take a look at an example of the lazy initialization of a database connection.

As always, we'll start by declaring an interface:

```
type
  IDatabaseConnector = interface
  ['{8E00247F-F910-41C1-9122-523F2CB6E5CB}']
    procedure Connect(const aName: string);
  end;
```

This is just a demo, so we won't be making real database connections, but we'll simulate it by causing a bit of a delay when pretending to "connect." So, given that, here is an implementation of our `IDatabaseConnector` interface:

```
  TDatabaseConnector = class(TInterfacedObject, IDatabaseConnector)
  private
    FConnected: Boolean;
  public
    constructor Create;
    procedure Connect(const aName: string);
    property Connected: Boolean read FConnected write FConnected;
  end;

constructor TDatabaseConnector.Create;
begin
  inherited Create;
  FConnected := False;
  Connect(Self.ClassName);
end;

procedure TDatabaseConnector.Connect(const aName: string);
begin
  if not Connected then
  begin
    WriteLn('Now connecting with ', aName);
    Sleep(3000);
    WriteLn('Connected!  Sorry I took so long!');
    Connected := True;
  end;
end;
```

This class implements the `IDatabaseConnector` interface, but takes a bit of time to connect. It "connects" by writing out to the console, waiting three seconds, and then writing again to the console that it is completed. Again, this is a demo connection, but it is sufficient for our purposes, as you shall see.

The real fun starts when we declare this type in a class that actually uses it. For instance, here's a class, `TDatabaseConnectionManager`, that accepts an `IDatabaseC-onnector` parameter in the constructor, which populates a field in the object.

```
  TDatabaseConnectionManager = class
  private
    FDatabaseConnector: IDatabaseConnector;
  public
    constructor Create(aDatabaseConnector: IDatabaseConnector);
  end;

constructor TDatabaseConnectionManager.Create(aDatabaseConnector: IDatabaseConnector);
begin
  inherited Create;
  FDatabaseConnector := aDatabaseConnector;
end;
```

This class, when created and passed an instance of `IDatabaseConnector`, will store that instance away for later use. But if we register everything with the Container:

```
procedure RegisterStuff(aContainer: TContainer);
begin
  aContainer.RegisterType<TDatabaseConnector, IDatabaseConnector>;
  aContainer.RegisterType<TDatabaseConnectionManager>;
  aContainer.Build;
end;
```

the implementation of `IDatabaseConnector` will be created automatically by the Container. But what if you don't want that to happen? Well, you can declare the variable a little differently:

```
  TDatabaseConnectionManagerLazy = class
  private
    FDatabaseConnector: Lazy<IDatabaseConnector>;
  public
    constructor Create(aDatabaseConnector: Lazy<IDatabaseConnector>);
    procedure ConnectToDatabase;
  end;

constructor TDatabaseConnectionManagerLazy.Create(aDatabaseConnector: Lazy<IDatabaseConnector>);
begin
  inherited Create;
  FDatabaseConnector := aDatabaseConnector;
end;

procedure TDatabaseConnectionManagerLazy.ConnectToDatabase;
begin
  FDatabaseConnector.Value.Connect(Self.ClassName);
end;
```

The only difference here is the declaration of `FDatabaseConnector`, which is declared as `Lazy<IDatabaseConnector>` instead of just `IDatabaseConnector`. The same is true for the parameter to the constructor. By declaring it as `Lazy`, it instructs the Container to create the connection on demand, rather than right away. That demand occurs when you ask for the `Value` property of the lazily-initialized variable.

Let's exercise all this stuff and see how it works.

Here is a procedure called `Main` that gets called by the `DPR` file:

```
procedure Main(aContainer: TContainer);
var
  DatabaseConnectionManager: TDatabaseConnectionManager;
  DatabaseConnectionManagerLazy: TDatabaseConnectionManagerLazy;
begin
  aContainer.RegisterType<TDatabaseConnector, IDatabaseConnector>;
  aContainer.RegisterType<TDatabaseConnectionManager>;
  aContainer.RegisterType<TDatabaseConnectionManagerLazy>;
  aContainer.Build;

  WriteLn('Everything is registered');
  ReadLn;

  WriteLn('About to create DatabaseConnectionManager');
  DatabaseConnectionManager := aContainer.Resolve<TDatabaseConnectionManager>;

  WriteLn('Note that Connection is made without anything being done on your part.');
  WriteLn('The connection occurs as part of the magic of the Container.');
  WriteLn('All Done');
  WriteLn;
  ReadLn;

  WriteLn('About to create DatabaseConnectionManagerLazy');
  DatabaseConnectionManagerLazy := aContainer.Resolve<TDatabaseConnectionManagerLazy>;

  WriteLn('Note that connection is not made until specifically asked for by you hitting Return.');
  ReadLn;
  WriteLn('Okay, now you have asked for the connection, and it will be made');
  DatabaseConnectionManagerLazy.ConnectToDatabase;

  WriteLn;
  WriteLn('All Done');
  WriteLn;
end;
```

This is a bit tricky to demo, so we'll take it step-by-step.

- First, everything is registered: the `TDatabaseConnector` class as implementing the IDatabaseConnector interface and the two classes that use the interface, one "regularly" and one "lazily."

- Once that happens, the application reports that everything is registered and calls ReadLn so you can see that all is registered and waiting for use.
- Then, when you hit the Enter key, it tells you it's about to create a TDatabaseConnectionManager and does so.
- At this point, you should see the connection being made. There is no delay – the connection is made right way, even before you do anything. This happens because the Container automatically creates everything upon the call to Build. Note it takes three seconds for the connection to be made as we simulate a delay in connecting.
- Next up, though, is TDatabaseConnectionManagerLazy. This class declares the database connection as Lazy, and thus it isn't created until you specifically ask for it. We can Resolve an instance of it via the Container *without* the Container creating and connecting. It only connects when we actually call ConnectToDatabase and first ask for the IDatabaseConnector. You can see this in action when you press Return and nothing happens until you press Return a second time.
- The application reports all of this to you as it is happening, so if you read the output carefully you can see what is happening as it happens. Remember, you need to wait the three seconds for the connection to be made. If you want, you can wait a really long time to make sure that the connection isn't made until it is specifically requested.
- You can tell – both times – when the connection is created because the application writes "All Done" to the console when it's finished.

There are only two basic differences between the two connection manager classes. The first one – TDatabaseConnectionManager – doesn't do anything special – it merely stores the reference to IDatabaseConnector for later use. It is the second class – TDatabaseConnectionManagerLazy – that has the differences. First, it declares its reference to IDatabaseConnector as Lazy, ensuring that it is only created when first referenced in code. Second, it does that actual referencing in the ConnectToDatabase method. (Note that the Lazy record has a property called Value which contains the actual reference to the lazily created instance.) It is at that point that the implementation is assigned and the class actually instantiated.

Registering Factories

Okay, that's all great so far. But you've likely noticed an inconvenient fact: All of our dependencies have been registered interfaces. What if our constructor needs strings or integers or other primitive types?

Well, the Container has a means of dealing with that. It enables you to register a "factory" to tell the Container how to create the class with constructor parameters that aren't registered.

A Coffee Maker Implementation

How about we imagine an interface for a coffee maker that manages what coffee gets made and how long the coffee brews. And of course, that coffee maker needs to know how to make coffee, hence the following interface:

```
ICoffeeMaker = interface
['{73436E03-EF65-44F5-9606-F706156CBEB5}']
  procedure MakeCoffee;
end;
```

But as we said, the implementation needs a coffee type and a brewing time, so we get this:

```
type
  TCoffeeMaker = class(TInterfacedObject, ICoffeeMaker)
  private
    FCoffeeBrand: string;
    FBrewingMinutes: integer;
  public
    constructor Create(const aCoffeeBrand: string; const  aBrewingMinutes: integer);
    procedure MakeCoffee;
  end;

constructor TCoffeeMaker.Create(const aCoffeeBrand: string; const aBrewingMinutes: integer);
begin
  inherited Create;
  FCoffeeBrand := aCoffeeBrand;
  FBrewingMinutes := aBrewingMinutes;
end;

procedure TCoffeeMaker.MakeCoffee;
```

```
begin
  WriteLn('Pour hot water over the ', FCoffeeBrand, ' so that it brews for ', FBrewingMinutes, ' minut\
es.');
end;
```

Now this class, as it stands, doesn't *need* to be put into the Container, but we can easily imagine the notion of, say, a `TKitchen` class that would take `TCoffeeMaker` as a dependency, and thus the class would need to be registered with the container for it to properly resolve. But again, the constructor takes a `string` and an `integer`. What to do?

Well, we can register a factory to tell the Container how to create the coffee maker. This type of factory takes the form of an anonymous method:

```
type
  {$M+}
  TCoffeeMakerFactory = reference to function(const aCoffeeBrand: string; const aBrewingMinutes: integ\
er): ICoffeeMaker;
  {$M-}
```

It's easy to think of an anonymous function as a factory. It's a "blueprint" for creating a specific thing, an implementation for `ICoffeeMaker` – in this case, `TCoffeeMaker`. Notice, too, that the blueprint's signature matches that of the constructor for our implementing class. This is not a coincidence, as you can imagine. For the anonymous method to be a factory as far as the Container is concerned, it must have `{$METHODINFO}` turned on. Once we have declared the anonymous function, we can register it as a factory with the Container:

```
procedure RegisterStuff(aContainer: TContainer);
begin
  aContainer.RegisterType<ICoffeeMaker, TCoffeeMaker>.AsDefault;

  aContainer.RegisterFactory<TCoffeeMakerFactory>;
  aContainer.Build;
end;
```

First, we do the normal registration of `TCoffeeMaker` against the `ICoffeeMaker` interface. Then we pass the `TCoffeeMakerFactory` anonymous function to the `RegisterFactory` method of the Container. The container is smart enough to look at the result type of the anonymous function in the Factory and figure out what interface it is supposed to resolve. Now we can get the information we need and resolve the factory to create the correct class:

```
var
  CoffeeName: string;
  BrewingMinutes: integer;
  CoffeeMakerFactory: TCoffeeMakerFactory;
  CoffeeMaker: ICoffeeMaker;
begin
  Write('What kind of coffee do you want to make? ');
  ReadLn(CoffeeName);

  Write('How many minutes? ');
  ReadLn(BrewingMinutes);

  CoffeeMakerFactory := Container.Resolve<TCoffeeMakerFactory>();
  CoffeeMaker := CoffeeMakerFactory(CoffeeName, BrewingMinutes);
  CoffeeMaker.MakeCoffee;
end;
```

This code is a bit interesting, and so you should notice the following:

- The `CoffeeMakerFactory` variable is of the type `TCoffeeMakerFactory`, or in other words, a reference to the anonymous function that is the factory. That line of code says "Get me the factory for a coffee maker." If you have multiple implementations, you can register them and retrieve them by name.
- The call to `Resolve` takes as a parameterized type `TCoffeeMakerFactory`. Note that it doesn't take the interface `ICoffeeMaker` as you might expect. It also uses the parentheses to tell the compiler that it's returning the anonymous function and not a `procedure of object`.
- Once we have a reference to the anonymous function, we can call it with the required parameters. It will return an interface, namely `ICoffeeMaker`. Now, this is a bit of Container Magic. The Container basically takes a look at the factory reference and finds a registered implementation of the result of the factory function that has a constructor that matches the factory's method signature. It then creates that class with the passed parameters and returns an interface to the instantiated implementation.
- From there, you can call the `MakeCoffee` method of the interface and get the results you expect.

By the way, if you are really feeling adventurous, you can do all that in one line of code:

```
Container.Resolve<TCoffeeMakerFactory>()(CoffeeName, BrewingMinutes).MakeCoffee;
```

Now we have a class registered with the Container that can be resolved with its constructor parameters, whatever type they are. Nice.

But now you are thinking (I know this because you are really smart, and of course you are thinking this) "What if I have, say, two implementations of `ICoffeeMaker` and they have different constructor parameter lists?" That isn't a problem. You just need to do a bit more work. First, here is a different implementation with a different constructor parameter list:

```
  TCupCoffeeMaker = class(TInterfacedObject, ICoffeeMaker)
  strict private
    FCupType: string;
  public
    constructor Create(const aCupType: string);
    procedure MakeCoffee;
  end;

 constructor TCupCoffeeMaker.Create(const aCupType: string);
 begin
   inherited Create;
   FCupType := aCupType;
 end;

 procedure TCupCoffeeMaker.MakeCoffee;
 begin
   WriteLn('Put the ' + FCupType + ' cup in the coffee maker and press the "Brew" button');
 end;
```

This one is a "cup" style coffee maker that only needs the type of the cup in the constructor, so here is what our factory declarations look like now:

```
type
  {$M+}
  TCoffeeMakerFactory = reference to function(const aCoffeeBrand: string; const aBrewingMinutes: integ\
er): ICoffeeMaker;
  TCupCoffeeMakerFactory = reference to function(const aCupType: string): ICoffeeMaker;
  {$M-}
```

Here is how we register everything:

```
procedure RegisterStuff(aContainer: TContainer);
begin
  aContainer.RegisterType<ICoffeeMaker, TCoffeeMaker>('regular');
  aContainer.RegisterType<ICoffeeMaker, TCupCoffeeMaker>('cup');

  aContainer.RegisterFactory<TCoffeeMakerFactory>.AsFactory('regular');
  aContainer.RegisterFactory<TCupCoffeeMakerFactory>.AsFactory('cup');
  aContainer.Build;
end;
```

and here is how we call it all:

```
    Write('What kind of cup do you want to make?');
    ReadLn(CupName);
    CupCoffeeMakerFactory := aContainer.Resolve<TCupCoffeeMakerFactory>();
    CoffeeMaker := CupCoffeeMakerFactory(CupName);
    CoffeeMaker.MakeCoffee;
```

As usual, here is a list of things to note:

- First, the `RegisterType` calls have names, since there is more than one class implementing `ICoffeeMaker`.
- Next, note that the call to `RegisterFactory` has a call to `AsFactory` which takes as a parameter the name of the implementation for that factory. This is required so that the Container knows which implementation to associate with which factory.
- Finally, the rest of the code is what you expect. You get a reference to the factory (which of course is an anonymous method) and then call it, passing in the cup type that you asked for previously.

Registering Primitive Parameters

In the previous section we saw how you can register an anonymous function as a factory in order to create objects with arbitrary parameters in their constructors. In this section we'll look at a more direct way to do that by using attributes on the constructor itself. In effect, we can register primitive types by name and then resolve them using attributes and the container. Let's take a look at how this works.

Here is a simple person class:

```
type
  TPerson = class
  private
    FOccupation: string;
    FName: string;
    FAge: integer;
    function GetName: string;
    function GetAge: integer;
    function GetOccupation: string;
  public
    constructor Create([Inject('name')]aName: string; [Inject('age')]aAge: integer; [Inject('occupatio\
n')]aOccupation: string);
    property Name: string read GetName;
    property Age: integer read GetAge;
    property Occupation: string read GetOccupation;
  end;
```

It's nothing remarkable, except that each of the constructor parameters is tagged with an `[inject]` attribute. They have names attached as a parameter that will identify them to the container. These attributes will point to registrations of their primitive types in the container. Those registrations look like this:

```
procedure Main(aContainer: TContainer);
var
  TempName: TPerson;
begin
  Randomize;
  aContainer.RegisterType<TPerson>;
  aContainer.RegisterType<string>('name').DelegateTo(
                                   function: string
                                   begin
                                     Result := GetLocalUsername;
                                   end
                                   ).AsDefault;
  aContainer.RegisterType<string>('occupation').DelegateTo(
                                   function: string
                                   begin
                                     Result := 'plumber'; // This could be retrieved from anywhere, of\
 course.

                                   end
                                   );

  aContainer.RegisterType<integer>('age').DelegateTo(
                                   function: integer
                                   begin
                                     Result := Random(100);
                                   end
                                   );
  aContainer.Build;
```

```
  TempName := aContainer.Resolve<TPerson>;
  WriteLn(TempName.Name, ' is ', TempName.Age, ' years old', ' and is a ', TempName.Occupation);
  ReadLn;
end;
```

There should be nothing unfamiliar here – you probably can figure out what is going on. The types being registered are primitives – two strings and an integer – and they are registered using the same string values we saw in the attributes. We then call `DelegateTo` to define an anonymous function that tells the container how to obtain the strings and the integer. (Note that we use the call `GetLocalUserName` from the previous chapter to get the name value.)

The difference here from all the code up to this point is that we are registering primitive types. Previously, we've registered classes, but here we register arbitrary primitive types. You can register any type that you like as long as you provide a name for the registration and an anonymous method to tell the container what the value of the primitive should be. As shown, you then label the parameters (they could be parameters on a method if you like) and the values are automatically set for us by the Container. Now you have another way of making a class completely resolvable inside the container.

Attributes

I start this section assuming that you know how attributes work in Delphi. (If not, feel free to read all about them in my book, "Coding in Delphi".) The Spring for Delphi framework provides a number of attributes that can be used in place of registration calls.

`[Inject]` Attribute

The Spring4D framework defines the attribute class `InjectAttribute`. This, of course, results in the `[Inject]` attribute. This attribute allows you to label any number of language elements in a class, including constructors, methods, properties, and parameters. (It also allows you to tag fields with it, but as we'll see in the next section, Field Injection is an anti-pattern.)

When a member is so tagged, it is the equivalent of adding the `Injectxxxx` methods to the class/interface registration calls. Thus, the purpose of the `[Inject]` attribute is to register a given class member as being injected into the container based on its type.

Consider the following code:

```
type

  IHorse = interface
  ['{BDBB0FE7-D369-4EC7-B2A0-FC012136B87E}']
    procedure Ride;
  end;

  ICowboy = interface
  ['{337002BB-2219-46A2-BF28-5CFD8A6873AD}']
    procedure SetHorse(aValue: IHorse);
    function GetHorse: IHorse;
    procedure DoCowboyStuff;
    property Horse: IHorse read GetHorse write SetHorse;
  end;

  THorse = class(TInterfacedObject, IHorse)
  public
    procedure Ride;
  end;

  TCowboy = class(TInterfacedObject, ICowboy)
  private
    FHorse: IHorse;
    procedure SetHorse(aValue: IHorse);
    function GetHorse: IHorse;
  public
    procedure DoCowboyStuff;
    property Horse: IHorse read GetHorse write SetHorse;
  end;

procedure BeACowboy(aContainer: TContainer);

implementation

procedure BeACowboy(aContainer: TContainer);
var
  Cowboy: ICowboy;
begin
  Cowboy := aContainer.Resolve<ICowboy>;
  Cowboy.DoCowboyStuff;
end;

procedure TCowboy.DoCowboyStuff;
begin
```

```
  WriteLn('Yippee Kay Yay!');
  Horse.Ride;
end;

function TCowboy.GetHorse: IHorse;
begin
  Result := FHorse;
end;

procedure TCowboy.SetHorse(aValue: IHorse);
begin
  FHorse := aValue;
end;

procedure THorse.Ride;
begin
  WriteLn('Gallop along the prairie!');
end;
```

and the registration code:

```
procedure RegisterStuff(aContainer: TContainer);
begin
  aContainer.RegisterType<ICowboy, TCowboy>.InjectProperty('Horse');
  aContainer.RegisterType<THorse, IHorse>;
  aContainer.Build;
end;
```

There is nothing in this code that shouldn't be familiar. The "work" gets done in the registration code with the call to `InjectProperty`. That tells the Container that there will be a property named 'Horse' that will be resolved by the given registration call. This allows you to never call `Create` anywhere in your class and instead let the Container do that work for you.

Now, you can do almost exactly the same thing with the following:

```
TCowboy = class(TInterfacedObject, ICowboy)
private
  FHorse: IHorse;
  procedure SetHorse(aValue: IHorse);
  function GetHorse: IHorse;
public
  procedure DoCowboyStuff;
  [Inject]
  property Horse: IHorse read GetHorse write SetHorse;
end;
```

and then simplify the registration as follows:

```
procedure RegisterStuff(aContainer: TContainer);
begin
  aContainer.RegisterType<TCowboy, ICowboy>;
  aContainer.RegisterType<THorse, IHorse>;
  aContainer.Build;
end;
```

I say "almost" the same thing, because when you use the attribute, you specify precisely which property you want to associate with the `IHorse` registration. If you use `InjectProperty`, the Container will associate that with any property on any class registered with the container that has a property named "Horse" of type `IHorse`. The attribute, on the other hand, limits the association to the property tagged with the attribute. This is a subtle but important difference.

Lifetime Attributes

Earlier, we discussed how the Container can be instructed to manage the lifetime of the instances that it returns and assigns for you. As I showed you then, this was done with a call during the registration process:

```
Container.RegisterType<IWeapon, TSword>.AsSingleton;
```

This code tells the container to always return the same instance of `TSword` whenever it retrieves an implementation of `TSword`. However, you can do the same thing with the `[Singleton]` attribute by attaching it to the `TSword` class:

```
[Singleton]
TSword = class(TInterfacedObject, IWeapon)
  procedure Wield;
end;
```

This will tell the Container that the implementation for `IWeapon` should be a singleton – that is, when the Container provides an instance of `IWeapon`, it should always return the exact same instance.

Conclusion

The Spring4D Dependency Injection container is quite powerful and capable. It can do more than merely match up interfaces and implementations, as we've seen.

Dependency Injection Anti-Patterns

So far, I've tried to show you good patterns and practices for doing Dependency Injection and for using the Dependency Injection Container. There are definitely correct ways that things should be done. And conversely, there are definitely ways that things shouldn't be done. This chapter covers some of these wrong ways – commonly called anti-patterns – that you may be tempted to use but should not. These anti-patterns are ones that have been tried but have shown to be wanting in producing clean, good, well-written code.

Service Locator

Easily the most well-known, most controversial, and most abused anti-pattern is the `ServiceLocator` anti-pattern. I call it well-known and controversial because for a long time `ServiceLocator` was actually accepted as a useful pattern for doing Dependency Injection. I call it abused because people still use it and believe it to be a useful pattern. I'll argue here that `ServiceLocator` is indeed an anti-pattern and that you should not be using it in your applications.

`ServiceLocator` is tempting. It's super easy to replace your calls to create with a call to `ServiceLocator.Resolve<IMyInterface>`. It's really natural to use the `ServiceLocator` whenever you need an implementation of an interface.

But as we've seen, `ServiceLocator` isn't needed. The Container can do 99% of the work that you are tempted to use the `ServiceLocator` for. Because the Container can automatically resolve any registered dependency that another registered class may have, you can use the `ServiceLocator` only once at the root of your application. The Container is fully capable of wiring up your entire object graph before the application ever starts. You do need that one resolve call at the root of your application, but it becomes a small price to pay for the huge benefit that the Container brings.

There are several further reasons why the `ServiceLocator` should be avoided.

- The `ServiceLocator` is a singleton, and singletons are global variables. Global variables are to be avoided at all costs.
- If you use the `ServiceLocator` as a replacement for your `Create` calls, you are in effect causing the Container to be nothing more than a big bucket of global variables. If you can grab any class instance from anywhere in your application, you are using the Container as such, and as I've said, global variables should be avoided.
- Using the `ServiceLocator` instead of passing dependencies hides those dependencies. One of the main purposes of Constructor Injection is to declare openly the dependencies of a class. If you use the `ServiceLocator` to create dependencies instead of passing them into a class, you subvert the benefits of constructor injection.
- By using the `ServiceLocator`, you create a runtime error instead of a compile-time error, and compile-time errors are vastly preferable. Constructor Injection used improperly will result in a compiler error. Using the `ServiceLocator` improperly will result in a run-time error. You should prefer the former.
- When you use the `ServiceLocator` you don't take advantage of the composability of the Container. The Container can be set up to properly compose your object graph. It can even be set up to provide different compositions for different reasons. But if you simply snatch implementations randomly out of the Container with `ServiceLocator`, you lose all the benefits of using the Container to compose your objects correctly.

All in all, the `ServiceLocator` should be viewed as an anti-pattern and avoided. Instead, rely on the container to resolve all your objects and make a single `Resolve` call at the composite root of your application. It's very tempting to use it because it seems on the surface like a very useful technique, but as we've seen, that temptation is but Fool's Gold and actually leads to trouble.

Field Injection

What is Field Injection

Field Injection is a type of Dependency Injection where you inject a dependency by setting a field value on a class. Here is a simple, explanatory example:

```
unit uFieldInjection;

interface

uses
      Spring.Container.Common
    ;

type
  IBrake = interface
  ['{74DBE39C-F52F-42C4-B7CB-8009F7EDF1E1}']
    procedure StopVehicle;
  end;

  IEngine = interface
  ['{0BC34CC8-DE81-4073-9CA4-A160CFB9A64A}']
    procedure PropelVehicle;
  end;

  ICar = interface
  ['{B2C1C9FB-E388-4F0B-9197-2BCAB5A2A396}']
    procedure Drive;
  end;

  TBrakes = class(TInterfacedObject, IBrake)
    procedure StopVehicle;
  end;

  TEngine = class(TInterfacedObject, IEngine)
    procedure PropelVehicle;
  end;

  TCar = class(TInterfacedObject, ICar)
  private
    FBrakes: IBrake;
    [Inject]
    FEngine: IEngine;
  public
    procedure Drive;
  end;

procedure MakeCarGo(aContainer: TContainer);
```

```
implementation

uses
    Spring.Container
  ;

procedure MakeCarGo(aContainer: TContainer);
var
  Car: ICar;
begin
  Car := aContainer.Resolve<ICar>;
  Car.Drive;
end;

procedure TBrakes.StopVehicle;
begin
  WriteLn('Step on the brake pedal and make the car stop');
end;

procedure TEngine.PropelVehicle;
begin
  WriteLn('Burn gas and make the car go');
end;

procedure TCar.Drive;
begin
  FEngine.PropelVehicle;
  FBrakes.StopVehicle;
end;
```

and the registration code:

```
procedure RegisterStuff(aContainer: TContainer);
begin
  aContainer.RegisterType<TBrakes, IBrake>;
  aContainer.RegisterType<TEngine, IEngine>;
  aContainer.RegisterType<ICar, TCar>.InjectField('FBrakes');
end;
```

Here are some things to note about the above code:

- It uses Field Injection for two fields, `FBrakes` and `FEngine`. When registering `TCar` as implementing the `ICar` interface, it attaches a call to `InjectField` that registers `FBrakes` as a field that will be injected upon creation. To register the `FEngine` field, it uses the `[Inject]` attribute. Both techniques are exactly identical and do the same thing.

- Because `TCar` is registered in the container and there are classes registered for the types of the fields, everything gets "wired up" automatically and a call to `MakeCarGo` behaves as expected.

Why is Field Injection a Bad Idea?

Field Injection can be very enticing. It can seem "cleaner" than constructor injection because it requires less code. It can seem easy because all it takes is a single attribute. But do not be fooled – Field Injection is an anti-pattern. Here is why:

- It breaks encapsulation by allowing access to a private member. Breaking encapsulation is a big no-no in the world of object-oriented programming. So is messing around with private members. Fields are private for a reason and should be managed internally by the class, not by an external entity. Fields values are normally set either by a constructor or a setter method. You should not set a field value based on some value from outside the class. In our example above, the two fields are private, yet they get their values from the Container, which is allowed to access them. Not good.
- Alongside of the fact that it violates encapsulation, Field Injection also hides a class's dependencies. If you only know or view the public interface of a class, you won't see all of the dependencies that a class has, since fields are hidden away in private sections. You may not know that the dependency is even there. With constructor and property injection, the dependencies are there to be seen and known. With Field Injection, the user of the class may never see the dependency and may even try to use the class before making sure that the dependency is present for use. That is an access violation waiting to happen. A look at `TCar`'s public interface reveals no dependencies. The constructor takes no parameters and there are no properties that can be set. If all you had were the public interface for `TCar`, you'd remain blissfully ignorant of what `TCar` really needs and does.
- In addition, how do you test a class that has a private dependency? How do you mock that dependency? You really can't. When you use field injection, you are basically writing an untestable class, and that seems like a foolish idea.
- Field Injection allows for circular dependencies. If you pass a field value from some external entity, you can't be sure that the reference isn't creating

a circular dependency. Constructor Injection prevents this by never letting internal references "escape" to create a circular dependency.
- Finally, Field Injection, especially if you use it for many fields in a class, can hide the complexity of a class and make you think that the class is simpler than it really is. After all, what is another field? However, if you inject your dependencies via the constructor, they can soon pile up and it becomes obvious that you are violating the Single Responsibility Principle. It would be really easy to add `IRadio` and `ITransmission` and `ISeats` and a ton of other fields to `TCar`, all without having to do much but register the classes. The constructor would remain plain and all would *seem* well. But, alas, it is not. If you are designing a car, you are going to want to break out a pretty serious class framework to keep the `TCar` declaration very high level, with dependencies cascading down into lower dependencies and so on. If your car had a hundred parameters on the constructor, that would be unwieldy. It's not a good idea, but it can be less painful to have one hundred fields. But of course, each one of those fields is hidden and makes the class harder to test, so you should avoid those injected fields.

Bottom Line: Use Constructor Injection and Property Injection, and don't use Field Injection.

Constructor Over-Injection

I hinted at this a bit above when discussing Field Injection. Constructor Over-Injection is the tendency to continue passing references backwards towards the composite root in each subsequent class's constructor, causing those constructors to bloat and take on too many parameters. Imagine `ClassA` which depends on `ClassB`, which in turn depends on `ClassC`, and then `ClassD`, and so on. You could end up with a constructor that looks something like this:

```
constructor TClassG.Create(aClassA: TClassA; aClassB: TClassB; aClassC: TClassC; aClassD: TClassD; aCl\
assE: TClassE; aClassF: TClassF);
```

This is clearly not desirable, though one can understand how it might happen if one is assiduous in using Constructor Injection. If you find yourself doing this, it is time to take a step back and realize that your class hierarchy has issues, the primary of which is likely that your class is not following the Single Responsibility Principle. A class that takes that many dependencies, even if it is merely passing those dependencies through to other classes, is very likely trying to do too much. Look to break your classes into smaller, more focused classes that do one thing and one thing only. This should prevent Construction Over-Injection.

Constructor Over-Injection can also occur in a more subtle way. Consider the following code:

```
unit uOverInjection;

interface

type
  IBankingService = interface
  ['{E367001A-94D1-4694-A0B9-FB0B3FD822ED}']
    procedure DoBankingStuff;
  end;

  IMailingService = interface
  ['{ED17BB98-CC8C-4DBF-9466-C20F6BBC4AE2}']
    procedure MailPayrollInfo;
  end;

  TEmployee = class(TObject)
  private
    FLastName: string;
    FFirstName: string;
    FWantsMail: Boolean;
  public
    property WantsMail: Boolean read FWantsMail write FWantsMail;
    property FirstName: string read FFirstName write FFirstName;
    property LastName: string read FLastName write FLastName;
  end;

  TMailingService = class(TInterfacedObject, IMailingService)
    procedure MailPayrollInfo;
  end;

  TBankingService = class(TInterfacedObject, IBankingService)
    procedure DoBankingStuff;
  end;

  TPayrollSystem = class
  private
    FBankingService: IBankingService;
    FMailingService: IMailingService;
  public
    constructor Create(aBankingService: IBankingService; aMailingService: IMailingService);
```

```
    procedure DoPayroll(aEmployee: TEmployee);
  end;

implementation

constructor TPayrollSystem.Create(aBankingService: IBankingService; aMailingService: IMailingService);
begin
  FBankingService := aBankingService;
  FMailingService := aMailingService;
end;

procedure TPayrollSystem.DoPayroll(aEmployee: TEmployee);
begin
  WriteLn('Doing Payroll');
  FBankingService.DoBankingStuff;
  if aEmployee.WantsMail then
  begin
    FMailingService.MailPayrollInfo;
  end;
end;

procedure TBankingService.DoBankingStuff;
begin
  WriteLn('Doing banking stuff');
end;

procedure TMailingService.MailPayrollInfo;
begin
  WriteLn('Mail out payroll information');
end;

end.
```

This looks great. But notice that, while there are two dependencies passed in, one of those dependencies – `IMailingService` – isn't always used. `IMailingService` is, however, always **required**. The `TMailingServices` class is being "greedy" and asking for more than it always needs. A class's constructor should only ask for dependencies that it really needs, and not for dependencies that it only sort of needs. This type of Constructor Over-Injection should be considered a Code Smell. Instead, you might consider using some other method, such as a Factory, to get an instance of the mailing service.

We should also recognize this as a (simple but illustrative) violation of the Single Responsibility Principle. That is, the `TPayrollSystem` class is doing too much. It is doing payroll and mailing things. Instead, it probably should just worry about payroll and then have a dependency that does the worrying about "sending". In other words, there should probably be a notion of `ISendPayrollInfo` and then various implementations based upon what the employee wants – snail mail, email, hand-delivered, whatever. TPayrollSystem should not be concerned with how the sending happens.

Thus, there are two kinds of the anti-pattern Constructor Over-Injection. First, there is the passing of too many dependency parameters in the constructor (I start getting nervous when the number hits three…). This should cause a reconsideration of the class design in light of the Single Responsibility Principle. The second is the passing of dependencies that aren't used directly by the class, or dependencies that aren't always needed. This should be considered a Code Smell and refactored, as well.

VCL Components in the Container

I discussed previously the notion of Injectables and Creatables. Some classes – Creatables – should be created manually and not put in the Container. WI talked about how certain classes like RTL classes – TStringList, TList, TStream, etc. – were Creatables and shouldn't be registered in the Container. Well, another entire group of classes that should never be registered in the Container is any VCL control that descends from `TComponent`. This is particularly true for `TForm` and `TDataModule`. There are several reasons for this:

- VCL controls have their own lifetime management system and putting them in the Container causes confusion, both on the part of the developer and the Container, as to who owns the components and when they should be destroyed.
- Many VCL controls are visual, and as such, they need to be managed by their visual containers (such as forms, panels, groupboxes and the like). Putting these components into the Dependency Injectino Container mucks up these ownership relationships. The Dependency Injection Container and visual controls don't mix well and shouldn't be used together.
- It's hard. You have to jump through a lot of hoops even to make it work. Keep things simple and reserve the container for business classes and other objects that you write yourself to enable your application to work.

Multiple Constructors

A class involved with Dependency Injection should have only one definitive constructor. That constructor should declare all the dependencies the class requires. Remember, a constructor's parameters should be the definitive list of dependencies that a class cannot live without. If a class has more than one constructor, then it is declaring more than one set of required dependencies, and that doesn't make any sense.

Multiple constructors will also make it difficult, if not impossible, for the Container to resolve how to create a class properly. Even if all of the parameters are resolvable for multiple constructors, the question of which constructor the Container should select is left unclear. A DI Container could have specific rules for selecting one of multiple constructors, but that decision might not be clear to the developer. And changes to the class might result in a different code path, unbeknownst to the developer. Not good.

Mixing the Container in with Your Code

> First, I've been guilty of this one, and only recently recognized it as an anti-pattern when Stefan Glienke suggested it as such. You'll likely find demo code from me out on the internet that does what I'm about to tell you is the wrong way to do things. I have endeavored to clean up my demo code – the code for this book should be correct – and I hope that I have done so completely (I have a lot of demo code out there...). Alas – live and learn.

Mixing the registering your classes and interfaces with your code by putting the registrations in the `initialization` section of your unit is an anti-pattern. When you do this, you couple your class to the Container, and as we've discussed, you should avoid unnecessary coupling.

For example: Unit testing protocol states that you should test your classes in isolation. If you do your registration in the `initialization` section, you can't test your code without involving the Container.

Instead, create a separate unit and put your registration code in the initialization section of that unit, and then use that unit only in the `DPR` file by including it in the project. This will allow you to register everything that needs to be registered while keeping the Container decoupled from your code. The example code for this book illustrates this technique.

Conclusion

Just as there are right ways to do things with Dependency Injection, there are also wrong ways to do things. This chapter discussed some anti-patterns that are tempting but not a good idea when doing Dependency Injection. Stay away from them and you'll avoid many problems.

A Simple, Useful, and Complete Example

Introduction

Okay, we've had a lot of theory and a lot of basic examples, so now it is time to put it all together into a real, working demo that actually does something useful.

The following example is a simple application that allows you to view files. It's expandable in that you can write more file type viewers and add them to the application at design-time. By default, it provides a text file viewer and a viewer for the most popular graphics types.

And, of course, it uses Dependency Injection as its basic design pattern. The main use is via Constructor Injection, but I included some Property Injection as well.

> The code for this demo can be found at: http://bit.ly/NickFileViewer

Interfaces

Naturally, the application depends on interfaces and not implementations of those interfaces (have I made that point enough yet?). So here are those interfaces, in their own unit, of course:

```
unit uFileDisplayerInterfaces;

interface

uses
      Vcl.ExtCtrls
    ;

type
  IDisplayOnPanel = interface
  ['{C334B1AE-F562-4EA6-B98D-BB52F1CBE7A7}']
    procedure DisplayOnPanel(const aPanel: TPanel);
  end;

  IDisplayFile = interface
  ['{3437F0E6-2974-4C1A-BA07-2598A2774855}']
    procedure DisplayFile(const aFilename: string; const aPanel: TPanel);
  end;

  IFileExtensionGetter = interface
  ['{9E28B18F-3CDF-4F6E-B629-D3E02E0E0E6C}']
    function GetExtension(const aFilename: string): string;
  end;

  IFilenameGetter = interface
  ['{48E1FFD8-73EA-43DF-B722-4A86206BDFCE}']
    function GetFilename: string;
  end;

  IFileDisplayerRegistry = interface
  ['{7211F4E0-0E7E-4216-912D-069E21660DE1}']
    procedure AddDisplayer(aExt: string; aDisplayer: IDisplayFile);
    function GetDisplayer(aExt: string): IDisplayFile;
    function GetExtensions: TArray<string>;
  end;

implementation

end.
```

The application has three main dependencies:

1. **`IDisplayFile`** – This is the interface responsible for actually displaying the file. It requires the filename and a `TPanel` on which to display whatever it has to display.
2. **`IFileExtensionGetter`** – This interface is designed to get the extension from a given file which is needed to know how to deal with the file.. Our implementation simply calls a function call from `System.IOUtils`, but it could be determined any way you like.

3. **IFilenameGetter** – The purpose of this interface is to provide a means to get a file name to be displayed. In our implementation, the user is prompted through an open dialog, but a filename could be arrived at through any means, as long as the interface is properly implemented.

The File Displayer

Let's take a look at the main class that does all the work and takes the dependencies. It's a standalone class that uses Constructor Injection to manage its dependencies:

```
unit uFileDisplayer;

interface

uses
      Vcl.ExtCtrls
    , uFileDisplayerInterfaces
    ;

type

  TFileDisplayer = class(TInterfacedObject, IDisplayOnPanel)
  private
    FFilenameGetter: IFilenameGetter;
    FFileExtensionGetter: IFileExtensionGetter;
    FFileDisplayer: IDisplayFile;
    procedure ClearPanelChildren(const aPanel: TPanel);
  public
    constructor Create(aFilenameGetter: IFilenameGetter; aFileExtensionGetter: IFileExtensionGetter);
    procedure DisplayOnPanel(const aPanel: TPanel);
  end;

implementation

uses
      System.Classes,
      uFileDisplayerRegistry
    ;

procedure TFileDisplayer.ClearPanelChildren(const aPanel: TPanel);
var
  Component: TComponent;
  i: integer;
begin
  for i := 0 to aPanel.ControlCount - 1 do
  begin
    Component := aPanel.Controls[i] as TComponent;
```

```
    Component.Free;
  end;
end;

constructor TFileDisplayer.Create(aFilenameGetter: IFilenameGetter; aFileExtensionGetter: IFileExtensi\
onGetter);
begin
  inherited Create;
  FFilenameGetter := aFilenameGetter;
  FFileExtensionGetter := aFileExtensionGetter;
end;

procedure TFileDisplayer.DisplayOnPanel(const aPanel: TPanel);
var
  LExt: string;
  LFilename: string;
begin
  ClearPanelChildren(aPanel);
  LFilename := FFilenameGetter.GetFilename;
  LExt := FFileExtensionGetter.GetExtension(LFilename);
  FFileDisplayer := FileDisplayerRegistry.GetDisplayer(LExt);
  FFileDisplayer.DisplayFile(LFilename, aPanel);
end;

end.
```

As usual, let's take a look at some things to note about the above code:

- The class `TFileDisplayer` implements the `IDisplayOnPanel` interface. I find this class to be quite beautiful. It asks for its dependencies, uses those dependencies to do a single thing, and does it all without actually implementing anything. Lovely.
- The constructor injects two dependencies as interfaces – an `IFilenameGetter` and a `IFileExtensionGetter`. Note that the constructor is very simple and merely stows those interface references away for later use.
- The `DisplayOnPanel` method is the one that implements `IDisplayOnPanel`, and it is the method where the dependencies are used. It gathers up the necessary information, gets the extension, uses the extension to get the right Displayer, and then calls `DisplayFile` on that displayer.
- It uses a class called `FileDisplayerRegistry` to manage the file viewers. We'll talk about that class in a minute.
- And that is it. All we need now is to implement displayers, and then we can hook this thin class in with the VCL user interface, and we have a functioning

application. This is nice, because we can loosely couple to the user interface and do most of the work by coding against abstractions. Note that the above class does exactly that. Every line of code in the class is coding against an interface. It doesn't know or care about how those interfaces are implemented.

Here's the implementation we are using for `IFilenameGetter`:

```
unit uFilenameGetter;

interface

uses uFileDisplayerInterfaces;

type
  TFilenameGetter = class(TInterfacedObject, IFilenameGetter)
  private
    function GetFilename: string;
  end;

implementation

uses
      Vcl.Dialogs
    , Spring.Container
    ;

function TFilenameGetter.GetFilename: string;
begin
  PromptForFileName(Result);
end;

end.
```

and for `IFileExtensionGetter`:

```
unit uFilenameExtensionGetter;

interface

uses uFileDisplayerInterfaces;

type
  TFileExtensionGetter = class(TInterfacedObject, IFileExtensionGetter)
  private
    function GetExtension(const aFilename: string): string;
  end;

implementation

uses
      System.IOUtils
    , Spring.Container
    ;

function TFileExtensionGetter.GetExtension(const aFilename: string): string;
begin
  Result := TPath.GetExtension(aFilename);
end;

end.
```

Both are quite simple and self-explanatory. Because they are implementing interfaces, you can easily implement them differently if you like, and as long as they meet the contract of the interface, they will perform just fine inside the application. That's why you code to an interface and not an implementation. If you want to get your filename from a database, you can do that without changing anything but the implementation of the particular interface.

Building Displayers

Okay, so the next interface we have to implement is `IDisplayFile`. This interface is the one where the real work gets done. For our application, we implement two – one that can display text files and one that can display graphic files.

Here is one that can display text – `TTextFileDisplayer`:

```
unit uTextFileDisplayer;

interface

uses
      uFileDisplayerInterfaces
    , Vcl.ExtCtrls
    ;

type
  TTextFileDisplayer = class(TInterfacedObject, IDisplayFile)
    procedure DisplayFile(const aFilename: string; const aPanel: TPanel);
  end;

implementation

uses
      Vcl.StdCtrls
    , Vcl.Controls
    ;

procedure TTextFileDisplayer.DisplayFile(const aFilename: string; const aPanel: TPanel);
var
  Memo: TMemo;
begin
  Memo := TMemo.Create(aPanel);
  Memo.Parent := aPanel;
  Memo.Align := alClient;
  Memo.ReadOnly := True;
  Memo.Lines.LoadFromFile(aFilename);
end;

end.
```

This class is simple (as all classes should be, right?). It implements the one method of `IDisplayFile` by adding a `TMemo` to the panel that is passed in and opening the text file into it. It couldn't be simpler. Another lovely example of a class doing one thing and doing it well.

Here's the very similar implementation for displaying graphics:

```
unit uPictureDisplayer;

interface

uses
      uFileDisplayerInterfaces
    , Vcl.ExtCtrls
    ;

type
  TPictureDisplayer = class(TInterfacedObject, IDisplayFile)
    procedure DisplayFile(const aFilename: string; const aPanel: TPanel);
  end;

implementation

uses
      System.Classes
    , Vcl.Graphics
    , Vcl.Controls
    , Vcl.Imaging.JPEG
    , Vcl.Imaging.PngImage
    , Vcl.Imaging.GIFImg
    ;

procedure TPictureDisplayer.DisplayFile(const aFilename: string; const aPanel: TPanel);
var
  Image: TImage;
begin
  Image := TImage.Create(aPanel);
  Image.Parent := aPanel;
  Image.Align := alClient;

  Image.Picture.Bitmap := TBitmap.Create;
  Image.Picture.LoadFromFile(aFilename);

end;

end.
```

Not much explanation needed for this – the class simply leverages the capabilities of `TImage` to enable the opening of any Bitmap, JPEG, GIF, or PNG file. Nifty.

Tying It All Together

We've used Constructor Injection to create a main class that manages things for us. We've implemented classes that allow us to view files. So now it is time to tie it all together.

Registering Extensions

First, we need a place to contain all the file viewers. Since we have a few file viewers and file extensions that tell us which of those viewers to use for those extensions, an `IDictionary` suits our purposes just fine. We can wrap it up in a registry, so that we store and retrieve the pairings. Since we want to code against an interface, we created the `IFileDisplayerRegistry` (seen above) that does the work we want it to do. Here's the implementation:

```
unit uFileDisplayerRegistry;

interface

uses
      uFileDisplayerInterfaces
    , Spring.Collections
    ;

type
  TFileDisplayerRegistry = class(TInterfacedObject, IFileDisplayerRegistry)
  private
    FDictionary: IDictionary<string, IDisplayFile>;
    FDefaultDisplayer: IDisplayFile;
  public
    constructor Create;
    procedure AddDisplayer(aExt: string; aDisplayer: IDisplayFile);
    function GetDisplayer(aExt: string): IDisplayFile;
    function GetExtensions: TArray<string>;
    // Property Injection:  We have a default displayer, but you can provide your own if
    // you want to.
    property DefaultDisplayer: IDisplayFile read FDefaultDisplayer write FDefaultDisplayer;
  end;

  function FileDisplayerRegistry: IFileDisplayerRegistry;

implementation

uses
      Spring.Container
    , uDefaultDisplayer
    ;

 var
   FDR: IFileDisplayerRegistry;

function FileDisplayerRegistry: IFileDisplayerRegistry;
begin
  if FDR = nil then
  begin
    FDR := TFileDisplayerRegistry.Create;
```

```
  end;
  Result := FDR;
end;

procedure TFileDisplayerRegistry.AddDisplayer(aExt: string; aDisplayer: IDisplayFile);
begin
  FDictionary.Add(aExt, aDisplayer);
end;

constructor TFileDisplayerRegistry.Create;
begin
  FDictionary := TCollections.CreateDictionary<string, IDisplayFile>;
  FDefaultDisplayer := TDefaultFileDisplayer.Create;
end;

function TFileDisplayerRegistry.GetDisplayer(aExt: string): IDisplayFile;
begin
  // never return nil.  If a Displayer is not found, then return the default one.
  FDictionary.TryGetValue(aExt, Result);
  if Result = nil then
  begin
    Result := FDefaultDisplayer;
  end;
end;

function TFileDisplayerRegistry.GetExtensions: TArray<string>;
var
  Extension: string;
  i: Integer;
begin
  SetLength(Result, FDictionary.Count);
  i := 0;
  for Extension in FDictionary.Keys do
  begin
    Result[i] := FDictionary.Keys.ElementAt(i);
    Inc(i);
  end;

end;

end.
```

`TFileDisplayerRegistry` class has three methods. Two are for managing the connection between the file extensions and the displayers that can display that particular type of file. You can both add and retrieve displayers. The third method is used to get a list of supported extensions for display to the user so they can know what types of files can be opened.

It also has a single property – `DefaultDisplayer` – that follows the Property Injection pattern. It allows you to set a value for a default file displayer that will be used in the event that there is no registered extension for the chosen file. The class provides a default displayer (seen below) that is returned when no registered displayer can be found. (Note that `GetDisplayer` follows the "Never return `nil`" rule by always returning an implementation of `IDisplayFile` no matter what). In addition, if you want to provide your own default file displayer, you can do so by setting the `DefaultDisplayer` property – just like we talked about in the Property Injection chapter. See, this stuff really does work.

Note, too, that the `TFileDisplayerRegistry` class follows the Registry Pattern and thus is exposed as a Singleton. The Registry Pattern pretty much calls for the resulting Registry class to be a Singleton, despite the fact that the Singleton Pattern has fallen out of a favor (it's really just a glorified global variable….). I did it this way for demo purposes – a more robust version of the application would manage the registration without resorting to this.

Here's the default displayer, which merely outputs some simple information about the selected file:

```
unit uDefaultDisplayer;

interface

uses
      uFileDisplayerInterfaces
    , Vcl.ExtCtrls
    ;

type
  TDefaultFileDisplayer = class(TInterfacedObject, IDisplayFile)
  strict private
    function GetFileSize(aFilename: string): Int64;
    procedure DisplayFile(const aFilename: string; const aPanel: TPanel);
  end;

implementation

uses
      Vcl.StdCtrls
    , Vcl.Controls
    , System.IOUtils
    , System.SysUtils
    ;

procedure TDefaultFileDisplayer.DisplayFile(const aFilename: string; const aPanel: TPanel);
var
  Memo: TMemo;
begin
```

```
  Memo := TMemo.Create(aPanel);
  Memo.Parent := aPanel;
  Memo.Align := alClient;
  Memo.ReadOnly := True;

  Memo.Lines.Add('Filename: ' + aFilename);
  Memo.Lines.Add('File Size: ' + IntToStr(GetFileSize(aFilename)) + ' bytes');
  Memo.Lines.Add('Creation Time: ' + DateTimeToStr(TFile.GetCreationTime(aFilename)));
  Memo.Lines.Add('Last Access Time: ' + DateTimeToStr(TFile.GetLastAccessTime(aFilename)));
  Memo.Lines.Add('Last Write Time: ' + DateTimeToStr(TFile.GetLastWriteTime(aFilename)));
end;

end.
```

To get all these displayers and classes registered, the project contains a unit named `uRegistration.pas` that has a procedure that does all the registration of the extensions and displayers. Note that you can register multiple file types against the same displayer:

```
procedure RegisterDisplayers;
var
  TextFileDisplayer: IDisplayFile;
  PictureFileDisplayer: IDisplayFile;
begin
  TextFileDisplayer := TTextFileDisplayer.Create;
  FileDisplayerRegistry.AddDisplayer('.txt', TextFileDisplayer);
  FileDisplayerRegistry.AddDisplayer('.pas', TextFileDisplayer);
  FileDisplayerRegistry.AddDisplayer('.dpr', TextFileDisplayer);
  FileDisplayerRegistry.AddDisplayer('.dproj', TextFileDisplayer);
  FileDisplayerRegistry.AddDisplayer('.xml', TextFileDisplayer);

  PictureFileDisplayer := TPictureDisplayer.Create;
  FileDisplayerRegistry.AddDisplayer('.jpg', PictureFileDisplayer);
  FileDisplayerRegistry.AddDisplayer('.bmp', PictureFileDisplayer);
  FileDisplayerRegistry.AddDisplayer('.png', PictureFileDisplayer);
  FileDisplayerRegistry.AddDisplayer('.gif', PictureFileDisplayer);
end;
```

I've registered a number of different text files that can be viewed using `TTextFileDisplayer`.

Registering Interfaces and Implementations.

Of course, the real magic happens inside the Dependency Injection Container. It is there that the interfaces are connected to their implementations, the objects needed are created, and everything is magically hooked up. Here's the registration code from the `uRegistration` unit:

```
procedure RegisterInterfaces(aContainer: TContainer);
begin
  aContainer.RegisterType<IDisplayOnPanel, TFileDisplayer>;
  aContainer.RegisterType<IFileExtensionGetter, TFileExtensionGetter>;
  aContainer.RegisterType<IFilenameGetter, TFilenameGetter>;
  aContainer.Build;
end;
```

Once this is done, you don't need to create a thing – the container will do all the work for you. Did you notice that the application doesn't create any of its business objects (save the singleton `TFileDisplayerRegistry`)? That's because the Container does all the creating and wiring together of all the interface references. (Remember when we talked about injectables? Well, most of the things in the application are injectables. About the only creatable is the `IDictionary` in the file extension registry.)

Connecting to the User Interface

Of course, none of this is useful unless you can expose it for the user. Here's a simple form at design time that will allow us to display files:

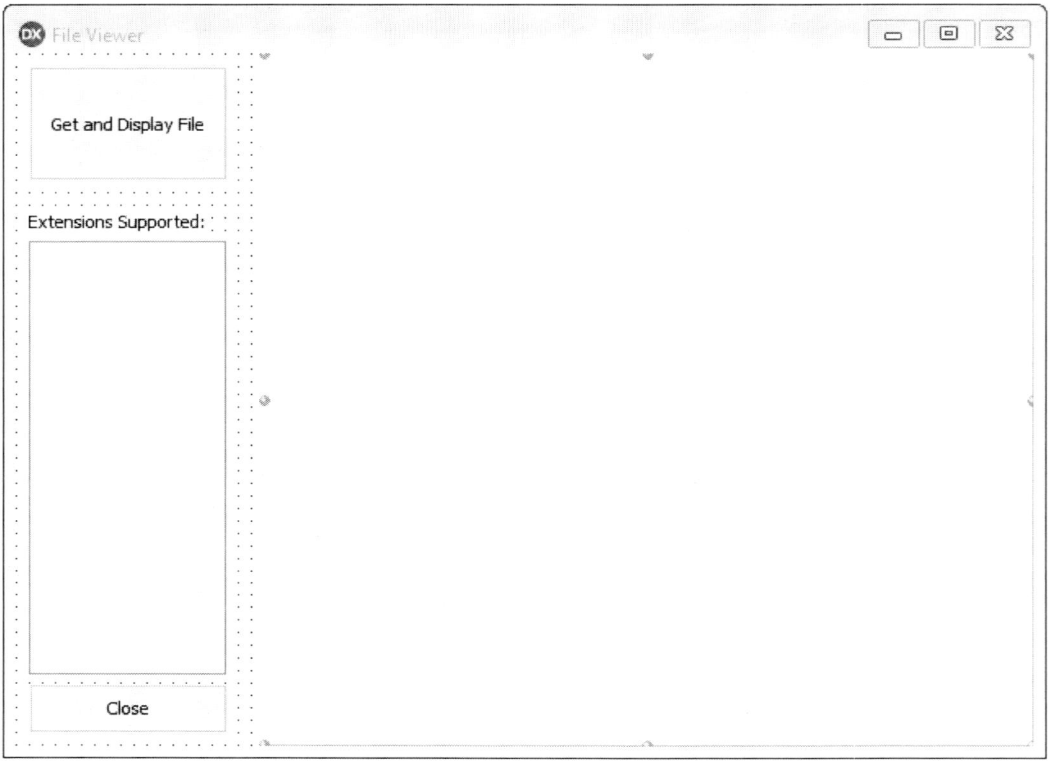

The File Viewer application in the Form Designer

The code to make it all work is pathetically simple. We've done all the heavy lifting already; now it is just a matter of taking advantage of our nice architecture to show a file in the application.

First thing, we add a private variable to the form of type `IDisplayOnPanel`:

```
type
  TFileDisplayerForm = class(TForm)
    Button1: TButton;
    Panel1: TPanel;
    Button2: TButton;
    ListBox1: TListBox;
    Label1: TLabel;
    procedure Button1Click(Sender: TObject);
    procedure Button2Click(Sender: TObject);
    procedure FormCreate(Sender: TObject);
  private
     FContainer: TContainer;
     FileDisplayer: IDisplayOnPanel;
  end;
```

Then in the form's `OnCreate` event, we add the following code:

```
procedure TFileDisplayerForm.FormCreate(Sender: TObject);
var
  Extensions: TArray<string>;
  Ext: string;
  s: string;
begin
  FContainer := TContainer.Create;
  FileDisplayer := FContainer.Resolve<IDisplayOnPanel>;
  Extensions := FileDisplayerRegistry.GetExtensions;
  for Ext in Extensions do
  begin
    s := Format('*.%s', [Ext]);
    ListBox1.Items.Add(s);
  end;
end;
```

Here we make our single call to `Resolve` (remember, we only get the one call) and fill up the list box with eligible extensions. Not much going on there.

The meat of things – and it's thinly sliced meat indeed – is behind the "Get and Display File" button:

```
procedure TFileDisplayerForm.Button1Click(Sender: TObject);
begin
  FileDisplayer.DisplayOnPanel(Panel1);
end;
```

That's it for the UI. Seriously. There's quite a bit of functionality in our application, but not a lot of it is tied to the user interface. And that's the way it should be.

And now here's the application displaying an image from my favorite album of all time:

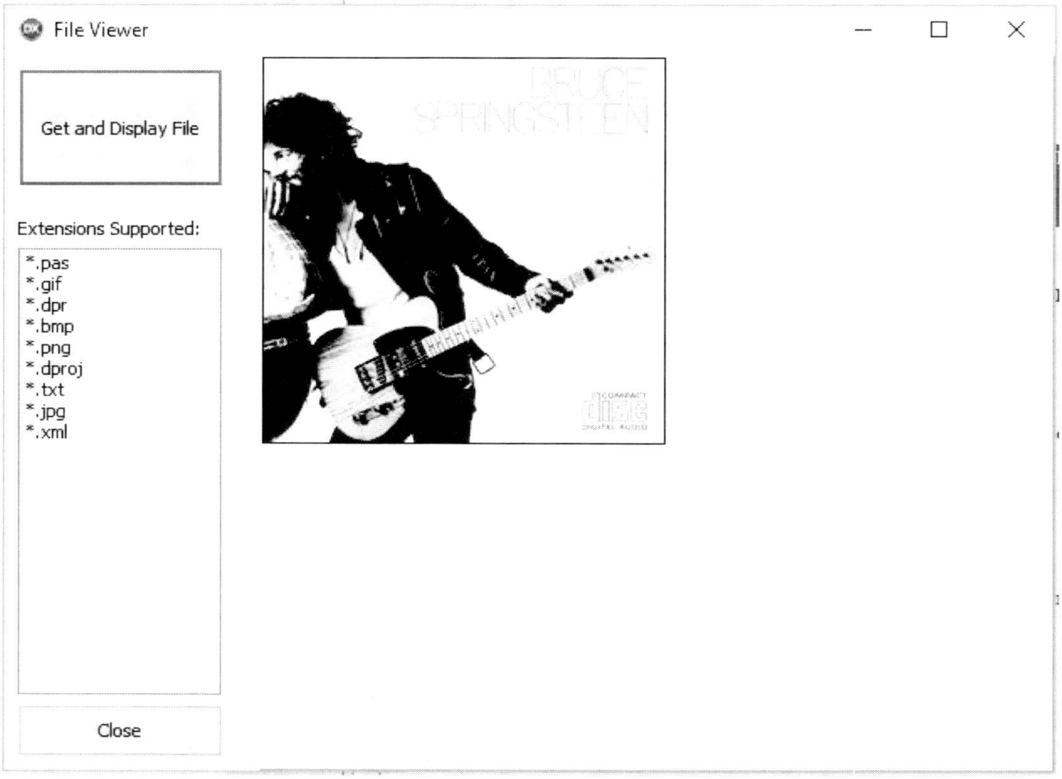

The File Viewer application displaying a file

Ways to Improve This Application

This application is a demo – it shows certain Dependency Injection techniques in action. However, because it is a demo application, it has left things fairly simple. I didn't want to cloud the main points to be made by making the application overly complicated.

Here are some things that you might consider adding to the application:

- Most obviously, you could write additional displayers for different kinds of files. Every file can be displayed in some way, and as long as you can place the results onto a `TPanel`, there is no limit to what you could add.

- Adding new file types currently requires a recompile. You could easily devise a scheme that allowed for plugging in file viewers dynamically.
- There is little to no error handling in the application, though it's likely that little needs to be added. The application does ensure that nothing is ever `nil`, so there's no need to check for that. However, the application doesn't, for instance, check to see that the file actually exists before it tries to display it.
- You could improve the file-getting implementation by allowing the user to select the extension she is interested in and filtering the search dialog box for those file types.
- You might consider replacing the file extension registry with an implementation that doesn't use a Singleton.

Conclusions

Here are some thoughts as we wrap up:

- All of the interfaces are in a single unit, so you can depend on that unit and not the units that implement the interfaces. Sure, you may end up with a bunch of units, but since it is so easy to look at each one and figure out what it does, it becomes a small price to pay.
- Each of those single units contains one class that does one thing. Following the Single Responsibility Principle keeps things clean and simple. The end result is that each class has a clear, understandable purpose. And even more importantly, each class is testable.
- All of the registration, both for the displayer registry and the Dependency Injection Container registration, is in its own unit. This is where things are coupled – the `uRegistration` unit is where the implementation units are used. That's the only "touch point" for interfaces and the implementations. That's about as loosely coupled as you can get.
- In the end, we have a clean, extensible, loosely coupled application. Maintaining, updating, and enhancing this application would be very simple. Adding the things described above shouldn't be hard at all.

I hope by now you can see the benefits of building your application with interfaces and Dependency Injection.

Final Thoughts

There you have it. I hope you have found this book useful. I hope that it has changed the way you think about building your applications. I hope you see the wisdom of coding against abstractions and injecting your dependencies, and I hope I accomplished what I set out to do in the preface.

Writing and maintaining code is hard enough without tangling everything together in a messy ball of yarn. If you could write your code in a way that makes things stand-alone, loosely couples those things together, and results in a powerful but easy to test and maintain application, you'd do it, wouldn't you? I hope that I've convinced you that Dependency Injection can do just that.

As I said in the preface – Dependency Injection is a very simple idea: Just hand your classes their dependencies, normally via the constructor. If that one basic idea is all that you've gleaned from this book, I'm happy. That simple idea can transform your code from the mundane to the sublime.

Dependency Injection has made a world of difference – all for the better – in how I write code. I implore you – let it do the same for you.

The Final Page

This page exists purely to make the book 131 pages long, so that Create Space will let the book have text on the spine. 131 pages is the minimum, and with this page, the book is 131 pages. Woo Hoo!

Made in United States
North Haven, CT
05 November 2026

21767762R10074